CW00545852

Views from an Indian Bus

snapshots of the subcontinent

Alistair Shearer

This is a sumptuous biryiani of a book, a feast for the imagination spiced with the mouth-watering details of what goes on behind the scenes in the world's largest democracy. In the twenty-first century India continues in her own inimitable style as a place where the ancient and the modern, the sacred and the secular stroll comfortably hand in hand, while the irrepressible creativity of her people turns the country into a realm where the extraordinary becomes the commonplace and the unthinkable a daily occurrence. Welcome to India: the land of unlimited possibility.

About the author

Alistair Shearer (www.alistairshearer.co.uk) was educated at Fettes and Magdalene, Cambridge and has been travelling to India for longer than he cares to remember. A cultural historian, he has taught courses in the art of South and South East Asia for the British Museum, Sotheby's, Christie's, SOAS (London University) and various art schools. Alistair regularly takes cultural tours to India; his latest incarnation is as an hotelier on the coast of Malabar in northern Kerala where he spends time writing each winter.

by the same author:

Effortless Being *(photos by Richard Lannoy)*

The Upanishads *(with Peter Russell & photos by Richard Lannoy)*

The Traveller's Key to Northern India

Thailand: the Lotus Kingdom

The Hindu Vision: Forms of the Formless

Buddha: the Intelligent Heart

Selections from the Upanishads *(with Peter Russell)*

Islam through Art

Buddhism through Art

Hinduism through Art

The Spirit of Asia *(photos by Michael Freeman)*

India: Land of Living Traditions *(photos by Michael Freeman)*

The Yoga Sutras of Patanjali

Praise for Alistair Shearer's books:

The Upanishads:

'A lovely decanting of this very old wine into a sparkling new bottle'

JOHN UPDIKE

'This is the kind of text that one keeps close at hand like an old, wise and compassionate friend'

RAM DASS

'An elegant and valuable contribution to the growing corpus of Upanishadic texts in English'

DR.KARAN SINGH

The Traveller's Key to Northern India:

'This is quite simply the most informed and the most literate guide to the great Indian keynotes. It is the *vade mecum* for the intelligent student of the subcontinent'

GEOFFREY MOORHOUSE

'Superb. A well-written, vivid and informative guide'

TRAVEL & LEISURE

'By far the best guidebook on India I have ever seen'

HUSTON SMITH

The Yoga Sutras:

'A wonderful translation, full of contemporary insight yet luminous with eternal truth'

JACOB NEEDLEMAN

Views from
an Indian Bus

snapshots of the subcontinent

❀

ALISTAIR SHEARER

With best wishes
Alistair Shearer

TRISHULA

Trishula Travel,
The Cottage, High Street, Laxfield, Suffolk, UK

First published in India by Trishula Travel June 2012
This edition published in UK by Trishula Travel November 2012

This book is available from
www.alistairshearer.co.uk

Cover and text designed by Andrew Bulbeck
Cover photographs by Alistair Shearer
Illustrations by Anthony O'Brien

Printed and bound by
Direct POD part of Lonsdale Direct Solutions Ltd,
Wellingborough, Northamptonshire, UK

ISBN 978-1-909424-13-5

For all further information about
Alistair Shearer's books, tours and teaching, please visit:
www.alistairshearer.co.uk

Contents

Introduction

INDIA is the Marmite of travel — you can't really be indifferent to it. The subcontinent is a strange and powerful place, not just a facile holiday destination, and a visit there can be a challenging experience that may well push you to think and feel out of your comfort zone. India has the habit of changing people, and for that reason many are instinctively afraid to go there, often citing 'the poverty' as an excuse. Of those who do make the journey, the lucky ones fall in love with the place and despite all the ups and downs a visit inevitably entails, will return time after time, preferring her above all other and easier destinations. But the subcontinent does not take to all who land on her shores; some will be chewed up and spat out and for those poor souls India becomes an unambiguous acronym: I'll Never Do It Again.

I have been interested in India since almost as long as I can remember. A great-aunt had been out there with her husband who worked for Coates, the cotton people. She had some wonderful tales of just the sort to captivate a young boy's imagination. There were spiders so big that when they crossed the piano keys notes rang out, and the cobra that was discovered lying curled on her infant son as he lay sleeping in his cot. Fortunately the bearer came with a long bamboo pole and expertly flicked the snake up into the air and away. Auntie Audrey had a house I liked: calm, comfortable and spacious and filled with what I would later recognize as the typical bric-a-brac of the 'India-returned'. Greeting visitors from its vantage point above the hall table was a small and rather sad stuffed alligator shot by her husband; some rooms had teak elephants of various sizes, each with little ivory tusks and toenails, that must always face the door; there were brass plates and candlesticks from Banaras, paisley shawls from Kashmir. Most magical of all was a wooden box that sat on the writing desk in her study. It was carved with writhing snakes and filled with tattered notes and worn coins bearing strange, squiggly writing and evocative names — *rupaiya, annas, paise*. I can smell them now.

Also, a favourite uncle had been out there in the army. When I was fourteen and senior enough to merit a study at boarding school, he gave me a rug for it which he had bought in the bazaar of the wild tribal town of Quetta. Uncle Bobby's rug has been my companion in all the many places I have lived since those distant schooldays. Magic carpet and fellow traveler, it lies in front of the fireplace in my Suffolk cottage as I write.

Then suddenly school was out, it was the 60's and flower-power India was in the air: incense, sitar music, patchouli; psychedelic deities and meditation were everywhere. After coming down from Cambridge I got a job at the then trendy Sussex University working in the library, where much shelf-stacking time was actually spent surreptitiously reading books on the subcontinent. I finally set off on the overland journey in 1969, and well remember my entry into the country. As I crossed the border from Pakistan in a horse drawn *tonga*, my senses were assailed. The sound of clipped hooves and jingling harness bells mixed with that peculiarly Indian aroma — a unique *masala* of livestock, incense, beedies, drains, clean sun-dried cotton and dust — and the sight of brilliant green parakeets that flashed through the trees above gangs of monkeys gamboling along the roadside. It was all unutterably exotic, and yet I felt as if I had come home. This was odd, as I had been brought up in Guildford and the leafy countryside of Surrey, neither of which had anything to do with monkeys or parrots, at least not in my childhood.

Hippy-trail backpacking matured with time into postgraduate study of Sanskrit and Indology, to be followed over the years by many, many returns to the subcontinent as writer, lecturer, photographer, art historian and leader of cultural tours. The latter were initially for the late and much-lamented Swan Hellenic, amongst whose clients were sometimes groups of museum 'friends' and university alumni. Swan's first Indian itineraries had been designed and led by Mortimer Wheeler, former Director-General of the Archaeological Survey of India and explorer of Mohenjodaro, the principle city of the Indus Valley Civilization. With his inimitable and rakish style, Wheeler continued his ground-breaking work by becoming our first media-archeologist. For me, lecturing on those Swan tours provided a very civilized way to accomplish several aims: travel, teaching, research and pilgrimage to sacred sites. Then, in the early 1990's, I began putting together and leading tours for my own small company, Trishula Travel, which is still happily in operation.

My most recent Indian project has been the creation of a retreat hotel on the coast of Malabar in northern Kerala (www.neeleshwarhermitage. com). Each day those who stay with us receive The Hermitage Times, a newsletter that includes a short topical item, and it is these pieces which have formed the basis of many of the articles in this volume. Though a number of them covered what was current news in late 2010 and through 2011, I'm confident that they have not dated unduly, as they cover subjects that are enduring as well as endearing. So my thanks are due to our guests at The Hermitage as it was their enthusiastic reception of the newsletter articles that planted the seed for this little book. More thanks are due to various friends who have sent me interesting snippets of Indian news. Foremost amongst these have been James 'the Colonel' Gibson and Suradeva Evenson, both of whom have been generous in their habit of ferreting out tasty tit-bits and passing them on to me. Thanks also to Andrew Bulbeck for his painstaking work in designing the cover and setting the text and to my old friend Anto O' Brien for providing the two illustrations.

I count myself hugely fortunate to have fallen in love with India at an early age — her people, her paradoxical, immensely subtle and wonderfully articulated culture, her landscapes. Of course, like any lover she can drive one to distraction; there is nowhere that can transport from one emotional extreme to another with such rapidity. The list of travelers who have fallen under her spell stretches unbroken from the days of classical antiquity. We have records from the wide-eyed Herodotus, the Chinese Buddhist pilgrim Fa-Hsien, Marco Polo, the eccentric Elizabethan adventurer John Coryat who rode an elephant at the court of the Mughal Emperor (and went on to introduce the fork to English dining tables), the disapproving French curate l'Abbe Dubois and the witty Mark Twain. And these are just the better known. While their author is all too aware that he is not in the same league as such august chroniclers, the essays that follow will at least confirm that India continues to be full of strange goings-on. Well into the digitalized twenty-first century she continues to be a place where gods turn green and girls marry frogs; maharajahs magnificate and communists believe in re-incarnation; where strange hybrids such as Indinglish and mythistory flourish, a three-eyed deity is a non-executive director of many local companies, a man tweets the world on a single grain of rice and much, much more. So, welcome to India: the land of dreams, the land of tales; a place where so many extraordinary things happen, largely because people still believe they can.

1

A highly spiritual matter

DESERVEDLY OR NOT, Kerala has the reputation of being the most inebriated state in India. According to official figures, 'God's Own country' dispatched booze worth over £80 million in December 2010, with New Year's Eve, labelled 'the drunkest day in history', accounting for almost £5 million of sales. Both the Prime Minister and the President of India reacted quickly by referring disparagingly in speeches to Kerala's notorious alcohol problem. Keralites protested loudly: the only reason the figures are so large here is that liquor sales are fully declared, whereas in other states they are partially hidden for political reasons. It is certainly true that the Kerala government has recently taken over the monopoly of alcohol sales and is cracking down on the importation of illicit hooch from central India. In the run-up to Christmas 2011, the authorities were on a high alert: vehicles, boats and trains coming into the state were spot-searched, bars and hotels busted. Even Ayurvedic pharmacies that use alcohol to distill medicines were raided. The legal alternative to hooch, known as Indian Made Foreign Liquor (IMFL) is a great revenue earner, as are the imported international brands drunk by tourists and toffs. Hotels selling these spirits have to pay a sobering £25,000 for their annual license.

But there is also strong public pressure to exert more controls on alcohol sales, especially from religious and womens' groups. At the very end of 2011 it paid off when the Excise Minister decreed that in future, the consent of local governing bodies will be needed if a new license is to be granted in their area. The anti-booze lobby hailed the measure as a triumph equal to the banning of *arrack* back in the 1990's. An always vociferous member of this lobby is the Kerala Catholic Bishops Council. But the fact is that wherever Christians have a presence in India, there is drink. And in Kerala the Christian community is ancient — founded by the doubting apostle Thomas it is the oldest outside Palestine — and large, forming approximately a third of the population. It is also wealthy, for it was usually the Christians and Jews who profited from the spice trade, rather than Hindus or Muslims. The orthodox wings of these latter two religious groups, both ostensibly teetotal, have been known to

1

point out that the Christian devotion to alcohol is hardly surprising — is not their central religious ritual a slug of blood-red liquor? Another perennially powerful lobby group in Kerala is the Communist block. Their hues of red may be as various as the communion wines but, at least according to their enemies, they are uniform in their atheism, secularism and fondness for a good drink. Example: the district collector of Calicut recently took the unprecedented step of banning all booze sales at a public holiday — a great success, as there were none of the usual alcohol-related problems. But alas, also no state revenue; he was transferred a few days later.

Historically, India's leading politicians have been mixed in their attitude to the demon drink. Her first Prime Minister, the socialist Pandit Nehru was Westernised and secular, but he still forbad the serving of alcohol on Republic Day and Independence Day celebrations. On the other hand, his enforced colleague the dapperly-suited Mohammed Ali Jinnah, leader of the conservative Muslim League and founder of Pakistan, was known to display strong similarities to both chimneys and fish. A later Indian premier, the pious Moraji Desai, was vehement in his opposition to alcohol, though his naturopathic habit of drinking his own urine each morning gave rise to many jokes on the Delhi cocktail party circuit that are unprintable in a wholesome family publication such as this.

The Indian Constitution vows 'to bring about the prohibition of intoxicating drinks and drugs that are injurious to health.' In the capital city Delhi you have to be over twenty-five to be served in a bar and parts of India are still 'dry' on some days. In the 1990s, Andhra Pradesh imposed prohibition, but abandoned the policy less than two years later. But perhaps in memory of its most celebrated son, Gandhi's home state Gujarat is still fully dry. Parched tourists can get a drink if they sign a paper saying that as they are alcoholics, alcohol is a medical necessity for them, and wily locals do a similar thing with a doctor's certificate prescribing it to cure a specific ailment, (presumably sobriety). But the poor do not have recourse to such sophisticated tricks, and country hooch is smuggled in from neighbouring states at inflated prices. Much of it, dangerously under-distilled, is sold in little plastic bags called potlis for twenty rupees or so, which is less than fifty pence. Vijay Mallya, Mr. Kingfisher Beer and India's number one liquor baron, has the facts on his side when he argues that such a policy not only loses revenue but encourages bootlegging and ends up with people consuming 'unsupervised deadly cocktails which can claim innocent lives'. In 2009 157 people in the state capital Ahmedabad died, and many others lost their sight, after drinking such illegal hooch. The state has now passed a bill which provides stringent punishment for making, stocking, transporting or selling 'spurious liquor'. This includes the death penalty if fatalities are caused.

It is a confused picture. Liquor and alcoholic products in India are banned from direct advertising, yet complicated laws tax alcohol by volume rather than strength, which encourages the consumption of strong beers and spirits by those who seek the greatest kick from their often limited money. A further cultural ambivalence is observable in the shop-signs, still found all over the country, proffering 'English Beer and Wine'. Such a signboard not only distinguishes the goods on sale within from noxious fake brands and second-rate IMFL, but simultaneously serves subtly to disassociate the vendor from his poisonous wares by showing them to be foreign imports, i.e. not really Indian. There are places — usually major pilgrimage towns such as Varanasi, Haridwar and Mathura — where alcohol, along with meat, is officially forbidden as ritually and spiritually unclean, yet the traditional religious stimulant of *bhang*, a heady decoction of marijuana, is widely available. Opium is consumed in Rajasthan, where most of it is grown. But beyond these special cases, India is traditionally an abstemious culture, and until relatively recently unaccustomed to alcohol and its abuse. As a result, the pernicious social effects of drink, being very much the exceptions to the general rule, tend to stand out here more starkly than they do in Europe, whose cultures have been marinating in the stuff for centuries.

Following the publication of Kerala's lurching alcohol figures, a recent article in The Hindu wittily lamented 'the familiar progression from jocose, to bellicose to lacrimose to comatose'. The writer was Krishna Iyer, India's most respected high court judge, now retired. He finished in fine style with a subtle swipe at the ruling Communists, prophesying disaster as 'government merchants cynically flood the youth with liquor until blood colours streets and homes red' *(sic)*. No doubt many Keralites, shocked by such strong sentiments, rapidly reached for the bottle to steady their nerves ... Cheers everyone!

2

A little local history

CELEBRATIONS were recently held to mark the re-opening of St. John's Anglican Church in Thalassery, a town about 80 kms down the coast from The Hermitage and once an important base of the East India Company. The 150 year old Gothic building with its stained glass windows and massive doors has been totally restored, along with its cemetery where several important historical figures lie buried. Chief amongst these is Edward Brennan, an Englishman who was shipwrecked off the coast and decided to settle. He became the EIC Master Attendant — the official in charge of the running of the port, who had the authority of a magistrate if necessary — and in 1851 founded what is now Brennan College which recently became part of Kannur University. He died in 1859, leaving all his money to local charities.

The British had first established their presence in Thalassery in 1682, and soon anglicised the name to Tellicherry. They obtained permission to settle from the local ruler and the town became a springboard for the fledgling EIC in Kerala and was before long a major spice-exporting port. The Company had some catching up to do, as the spice trade had long been dominated by the Dutch. They were the first to map the seas of the southern hemisphere — up until then a completely unknown area — at a time when maritime charts, esoteric documents that often contained deliberate mistakes to mislead the uninitiated, were more valued by pirates than gold. The Dutch East India Company was financed by a system of public debt that allowed their government to borrow off its citizens at low rates of interest, not unlike a modern central bank. The result was a maiden voyage of 20 ships to the spice island of Java that realised a profit of 2,500% and the subsequent establishment of Antwerp as Europe's main exchange market and the most sophisticated and dynamic of her cities. Business boomed: nutmeg, for example, regularly reaped a 600% profit, many times the mark-up on cocaine today. Altogether the company was a model of efficiency; by the time it was wound up in 1796, it had averaged an annual shareholder dividend of 18% over a period of 200 years.

Such spectacular success made the Dutch widely envied in England, a spleen that was vented by enriching our language with such pejoratives as 'Dutch courage' (found in a bottle); 'a Dutch wife' (prostitute); 'Dutch comfort' (no comfort at all) and 'double Dutch' (meaningless nonsense). And surely only the stingiest would expect his fellow diners to 'go Dutch'. A more positive reaction to Holland's success was to seek to emulate it, and this is just what Elizabeth 1 was doing when, in 1600, she granted a group of 218 private businessmen a monopoly to get a share of the Indonesian spice trade. Thus was born The East India Company.

In time the EIC would become the world's first multi-national company, (the full story is well told in Niall Ferguson's *Empire*), but its beginnings stuttered. The first couple of trips to Java and Sumatra yielded little profit but en route the EIC ships attacked a Portuguese vessel and captured many Indian goods from it, including supplies of calico — light cottons named after Calicut, from where they were exported. This adroit little bit of piracy alerted the Company to India's potential as a source of trade, and well aware that the Indonesian archipelago was effectively policed by the better-armed and funded Dutch navy, the EIC decided to settle on the subcontinent as the second best option available and the place it could source its own spices in relative peace and quiet.

The particular Indian prize was the Kerala pepper (our word derives from the Malayalam word *pippali*) for in those days spices were not just an optional taste-enhancer. Unable to feed their cattle over the harsh winter, European farmers routinely slaughtered the beasts each autumn and used spices to preserve the meat. Their pungency had the added advantage of being able to disguise the taste of any that had gone off. Spices were so highly valued that they were accepted as payment of income tax, and even became a type of currency, from which we get our phrase 'a peppercorn rent'. Fragrant Kerala spices were placed among the flowers and herbs of nosegays used to block out the stink of London streets and in the mid-seventeenth century they were also used in the 'plague masks' that people hoped could protect them from the dreaded disease. Less dramatically, the ever-pungent Tellicherry pepper is still considered the best today and is much sought after by chefs around the world.

One of Thalassery's most celebrated residents was the German scholar and missionary Hermann Gundert, who ran the Basel Mission School here. His statue still stands in town. Gundert was one of those brilliant and indefatigable early travelers who took India to their heart. Only 22 when he left the Black Forest to preach the Gospel in Calcutta, he passed the time on the sea voyage out by learning Bengali, Hindustani and Telegu. Later he mastered Tamil and eventually spoke nine Indian languages. Settling in Kerala, he went on to produce the first English-Malayalam dictionary in 1872, translate the Bible into Malayalam, write twenty books in that language and found *Rajya Samacharam*, the first Malayalam newspaper. As a passionate and enterprising recorder of language and dialect, Gundert did much of his linguistic research just by hanging around the bazaar with his eyes and ears wide open. He soon realized that language and idioms become richer when the speaker is worked up over something, so, as he tells us in his memoirs, he would often go into the market and deliberately start an argument by accusing a shopkeeper of over-charging or a street vendor of short-changing him. Then he would quickly scuttle home to jot down the colourful expressions his little ploy had unleashed.

No doubt better known than Gundert is his grandson, the Nobel Laureate novelist Hermann Hesse. Both his parents had been born in India and did missionary work there, but it was his grandfather's influence that the writer particularly remembered imbuing him with a sense of universal tolerance and a love of India and things spiritual. The young Hesse himself was naturally contemplative and when his wife became schizophrenic and was hospitalized, he sought solace in long solitary walks in the meadows around his home in the Swiss Alps. Hesse went on to write many books to do with the inner life, the most celebrated of which was *Siddhartha*, a novella set in India and based on the life of the Buddha. It became something of a classic among the spiritual seekers of the 1960's, and in 1972 the underground filmmaker Conrad Rooks turned it into a movie, which was mainly shot in Rishikesh, a pilgrimage town on the Ganges where the Beatles had studied meditation with the Maharishi a few years before. The film starred heartthrob Shashi Kapoor as the young prince who renounces his throne to seek enlightenment, and contained a female nude scene which caused considerable controversy at a time when the Indian film censors did not permit even a kiss to be shown on screen. *Siddhartha* has been translated into Malayalam and Sanskrit by Thalaserry's Hesse Society, which has plans to publish editions in all of the Indian languages. Each year there is a literary get-together between the members of the society and their European counterparts, and the town is twinned with Hesse's ancestral town, Calw.

Thalassery has three firsts to its credit. First of these is what has long been India's national obsession: cricket. The game that combined British morality and muscular Christianity into the glue that was to hold the Empire together was introduced to the soldiers garrisoned in the EIC fort at the end of the eighteenth century by a professional soldier called Arthur Wellesley. He was the younger brother of Richard Wellesley, then the Governor General of India at a time the British were fighting the French for dominance in the subcontinent. After his time in India Arthur went on to gain fame as the 'iron' Duke of Wellington, carrying on the family tradition and winning the home leg by defeating Napoleon's European team at Waterloo. The subcontinent's first official cricket club was founded here in Thalassery, and a decent turf pitch was laid in the 1890's by a local tea-planter called Cowdrey. He was mad on cricket and had even named one of his sons after the world's most famous club by giving him the initials M.C.C. In time, Michael Colin Cowdrey grew up to play for Kent and England, fulfilling his father's wish by becoming one of the most accomplished batsmen, and probably the greatest slip-fielder, ever to wear the England colours.

Thalassery's second first is the Indian circus, which has always had strong links with the town. A local gym teacher in Gundert's mission school was so taken by a visit from what was then the only circus in India that he made a deal with its owner to supply it with acrobats. He set up his Circus Training School in 1901, and from then on the town became synonymous with circus skills. Performers and trainers from here are still very much in demand all over the country.

And then there are the cakes. It was here in 1883 that Indians first learned to enjoy European-style patisseries, initially made for sweet-toothed British ex-pats, especially at Christmas. Thalassery cakes are still India's tastiest. 2012 sees big anniversary celebrations of the first one baked and the beginning of a local industry which has continued to thrive while others such as coir, cashews and handloom weaving have dwindled despite generous state handouts. The highlight will be the creation of a 350 foot long cake, its icing decorated with the history of Kerala in words and pictures.

Cricket, circuses and cakes: together they have given this little place, with its attractive harbour and bobbing fishing boats, the title of 'the town of the three C's'. But, considering the Colin Cowdrey connection, perhaps the score should be increased to five, or even a six?

3

All that glisters...

TRAVELLING THROUGH THE paradisiacal lush green countryside of Kerala, one would imagine that the state must be a huge producer of foodstuffs. After all, you only have to drop a seed into the ground and it sprouts, right? Not so. In fact, Kerala imports almost all her food — milk, eggs, meat, those gleaming heaps of vegetables adorning the markets and even rice, wheat and sugar. Astonishingly, only 15% of the rice eaten in the state is produced here — the balance coming from Andhra Pradesh and north India — and barely 20% of the vegetables, the rest being imported from neighbouring Tamil Nadu and Karnataka. So it is almost entirely thanks to other states, and good relations with them, that there is enough food on the tables of 'God's own country'. Coconuts and fish are about the only things not imported, though the changing temperatures of Kerala's seas are displacing some of the latter — sardines and mackerel mainly — to India's north-east coastal waters.

One reason for Kerala's lack of cultivation is simply limited land availability. With its burgeoning population over 30 million, the state is divided between a densely populated coastal strip which is long (370 miles) but very narrow (average 20 miles wide) and the sparsely populated eastern hills growing spices, coffee and tea. Despite heavy monsoons that deliver on average about ten feet of rain a year, the water retention needed for crop irrigation is often difficult in the sandy coastal regions. From 1970 onwards, the Communist government, after various legal tussles with the Centre, set ceilings on large landholdings in order to redistribute smaller parcels of land to the historically disadvantaged. This process is still continuing today; indeed the government has just declared its intention for every citizen of Kerala to own land by 2015. One effect of this can be seen in the near-omnipresence of large houses with a fair-sized garden around them, an unusual pattern in India and one that limits space for growing food. Another factor is Kerala's educational record: a literacy rate that is the highest in the country and higher than that in the USA has lead to working people abandoning agriculture en masse. They move either to urban centres, where they purchase food rather than grow it or, very often, take their skills abroad.

Another view according to its critics, is that Kerala's government simply does not care about agriculture. They point to the fact that not only does the Agriculture Production Commissioner, one K. Jayakumar, triple up as 1) Head of Home and Vigilance Department (i.e. the terrorism czar), 2) Head of Inland Waters Department and 3) Head of the Temple Administration Department, he also has other jobs. One certainly demands time and attention: Chief Co-ordinator at the Sabrimala Temple site in south Kerala which has to deal with hundreds of thousands of pilgrims entering the state each winter; another, Vice-Chancellor of the Veterinary University, perhaps less so. Whether, like many multi-tasking Hindu deities, Mr. Jayakumar has several heads and multiple arms, is unclear. Another sign that the government may not be fully focused on agriculture is that the presumably important post of Agriculture Director has been left vacant for the last year. The Socialist Democrats, responsible for the agriculture portfolio in the current coalition government, were recently announced to be 'taking a look' at the problem to try to stimulate the sector.

They had better act swiftly. Many farmers unable to pay their debts are committing suicide in the hilly district of Wayanad, adding their numbers to the already shocking national average of forty-seven farmers who have killed themselves each day for the past 15 years. And here the banks must take their share of the blame. Since its liberalization in the 1990's the Indian banking sector has evinced some strange priorities: a government owned bank will give you a loan to buy a Mercedes at six per cent, while the same loan for a tractor costs fifteen per cent. Normal interest rates rise frequently and are currently a crippling eighteen per cent, while local agricultural credit organizations, cooperative banks which also loan farmers money, are equally inflexible. Critics see the situation as a glaring indictment of neo-liberal fiscal policies that prevent government intervention to ease repayment strictures or, in extreme cases, write off debts.

Part of the problem is the shape third world modernization is taking. Television consumer propaganda has lured many farmers into abandoning the tradition of growing their own food and being self-sufficient in favour of growing cash crops for the open market. Very often this crop is rice. The trouble with rice is that it needs water 24 hours a day, and part of World Bank aid packages stipulate that, to conform with free market policy, essential industries such as electricity must be privatised. In dry areas, if the rains fail water must be drawn from wells by electrical pumps, whose power comes not from the state, but from inflexible private companies. To pay their bills the farmers have to go to the money-lenders and are left without their own food, at the mercy of fluctuations in world demand and prices and chronically in debt. This is nothing new — we have seen it all before with soya beans in Brazil and cassava in Thailand — but it is new to India.

The effect of all these various factors is that Kerala is now effectively a remittance economy, living off foreign proceeds earned in Dubai and the Gulf states. The aim of many Keralites is to leave Kerala as soon as they can, earn relatively good money for a limited time, come home, buy land or develop their ancestral plot, build a nice home on it and… relax. In the early 1970's when the Gulf boom began, many Keralites were duped by unscrupulous middle men and ended up dumped in Karachi, where they are still stuck, unable to get visas home. Nowadays things are better; workers may be promised higher wages than they really get and are often treated badly by their hosts, but to many Keralites the astroturf of the Gulf continues to remain greener.

This pattern is particularly widespread in the historically disadvantaged Malabar, the northern part of the state, which contains a large Muslim population that feels at home in the Gulf culture. It accounts for the modern houses and continuous sprawl of building going on everywhere there. In the hinterland of National Highway 17 one finds some real 'Dallas palaces', huge compounds with private indoor swimming pools and the swishest of air-conditioning systems — very rare amenities in India. Even a medium sized Malabar town such as Kanhangad has three huge gold supermarkets and as many vast showrooms of electronic goods, Dubai-style, while several more such malls are being built.

This rapid pace of 'progress' has several immediate consequences. One is serious erosion in both coastal and river areas due to illegal mining of the sand needed for the hectic building programme. Another is that, just as small local merchants are being forced out by malls full of brand names, so the traditional skills Kerala once excelled in, such as wood working , are virtually unobtainable locally as the remaining few artisans move abroad to work. The Malayali looks at local employment only as a training period before he sets off overseas; some estimates say 2 million Keralites work abroad and another million in different parts of India, figures that chart the latest wave of a diaspora that, thanks to Kerala's tradition of good education, has long been well-established. There is the old joke that when Neil Armstrong landed on the moon, he .

found a Malayali sitting there waiting with his tea stall at the ready.

So nowadays an influx of labour into Kerala from less well-off states in the north-east — Orissa, Assam, Jharkhand, Bengal — is inexorably taking place. These migrants work in building and road construction, the plywood industry, plastic manufacturing firms, in brick kilns and in hotels, and they are all lured in their turn by the promise of wages that are better than those they could command in their own state. Kerala has become to these workers from the east what the Gulf is to the Malayali and researchers estimate there are now up to a million outsiders working in the state, though no official figures exist. Some small towns are totally dependent on migrant labour, but the instability of such a workforce, always ready to move on to where wages are higher, is not conducive to long-term social stability.

Education has long been Kerala's proudest boast, but now, whether academic or apprenticed, it is beginning to be valued much less, particularly in the historically under-educated Muslim communities. Why spend money on higher education for a child — and Muslims have more children than other communities — when he can go to Dubai and immediately earn more driving a bus than would a bank manager with over twenty years experience back home? Gulf returnees are unconcerned about paying inflated prices for everything from food to land; their wallets skew the local economy and bring real hardship to many of those who have no Gulf connections. Bereft of oil, Dubai has always been a warehouse for contraband, and the large flow of people and goods it now ships to Kerala is a smuggler's dream. Drugs, gold and huge amounts of fake Indian currency printed in Pakistan are part of a very lucrative trade; curiously, Kerala's customs, police and even her press all appear to suffer chronic eyesight problems as the goods pass through.

At least one local industry, albeit a bizarre one, has benefitted from the new pattern of working in distant lands: post-mortem freezing. In a country that traditionally practices rapid cremation for Hindus and even rapider burial for Muslims you can now find shops selling caskets fitted with internal compressors — aluminum ice coffins which will preserve the body of a parent or grandparent in the event of their dying while their children are abroad. The offspring can thus hurry home to catch a last sight of the beloved relative before they dematerialize for good.

But there is a more ominous wider context. Kerala has always enjoyed relative social harmony within her religious plurality. Cynics attribute this to the fact that the Christians, who are most numerous in the central part of the state, operate as a buffer between the Muslims in the north and the Hindus in the south. But increasingly in the north, the non-Muslim population is feeling disadvantaged by 'the Gulf syndrome'. Blatant economic imbalance never augurs well for social harmony.

So what Kerala's superficial gloss of development may mean for her long-term economic health and social cohesion is an interesting question. Looking on the positive side, given the inevitable global shift to localization of production and consumption, let us hope more of those large house compounds will be set aside for cultivation in the future. That way, 'God's own country' will be better able to live up to its name. It might even become what it appears at first sight to be: a self-sufficient tropical Eden.

4

A queen and her confidant

Thanks largely to the unlikely pairing of Dame Judi Dench and Billy Connelly, everyone nowadays knows of the close and sometimes tempestuous relationship between Queen Victoria and her manservant John Brown, the gruff Scot who befriended the monarch after the death of her beloved husband Prince Albert in 1861. Less people are familiar with her fondness for Duleep Singh, the son and heir of one-eyed Ranjit Singh, 'the Lion of the Punjab' who fought the Anglo-Sikh Wars in an attempt to establish his kingdom's independence from the Raj. Exiled from his native land, Duleep Singh lived in Britain as a country squire, first near Balmoral and later at Elvedon in Norfolk, before dying in Paris on his way to try to regain his throne in the Punjab. But a recent book reveals the Queen Empress had another Indian confidant from an even unlikelier quarter — a handsome young Muslim from Agra called Abdul Karim. Private diaries on which the book is based add weight to the suggestion that Victoria was probably far closer to this Indian subject than to her well-known Scottish one.

Abdul Karim was just 24 when he arrived in England to wait at table during Queen Victoria's Golden Jubilee year, 1887, four years after Brown's death. He was given to her as a 'gift from India'. Within a year, the handsome young Muslim was clearly a rising star at court, becoming the queen's teacher *(munshi)* in Urdu and also Hindi, in which her progress was sufficient for her to write diary entries in the language. Karim introduced his sovereign to curry, which rapidly became a regular part of the royal dinner menu. More importantly he also began to brief her on Indian affairs, giving her an informed insider's perspective on a country she never actually visited. But she certainly loved India at a distance: 'so bright a jewel in the crown' as she famously commented to Lady Canning, wife of the Viceroy. Victoria even created her own private India in miniature on the Isle of Wight — the Durbar Room at Osborne is filled with Indian art and artifacts. Such a feeling for the country must have owed something to Karim's influence.

In return, the Queen's *munshi* was named in court circulars, given the best positions at operas and banquets, allowed to play billiards in all the royal palaces and enjoy a private horse carriage and footman. He and his wife were given residences on all of the main royal estates in the UK and also land in India. Karim cut a dashing figure wearing a sword and his medals at court, and was permitted to bring his family members over from India to England. His father even got away with smoking a hookah pipe in Windsor Castle, despite Victoria's well-known aversion to tobacco.

Karim travelled around Europe meeting monarchs and prime ministers and eventually became Victoria's highly decorated secretary. In the years between his arrival in the UK and her death in 1901, the Queen signed letters to Karim as 'your loving mother' and 'your closest friend', sometimes even signing off with a flurry of kisses, something that was highly unusual at that time. It was unquestionably an intense — though no doubt perfectly proper — relationship between a young Indian man and a woman who at the time was over 60. As she once said "I am so very fond of him. He is so good and gentle and understanding... and is a real comfort to me"

So close were the two that the elderly monarch stipulated he should be among the principal mourners at her funeral in Windsor. She knew full well how this would infuriate her family and household, for if they had disliked Brown, they loathed Karim. Such was the level of ill-feeling that barely a few hours after the Queen's burial, her son Edward VII unceremoniously sacked the *munshi* and ordered that all records of the relationship be destroyed. Fortunately, Karim's personal diaries were kept in India by family members, and there they have stayed since his death in 1909. Until recently, that is, when they were tracked down in Karachi by the persistent efforts of British Indian researcher Shrabani Basu. Spanning his 10 years in England between Victoria's golden and diamond jubilees, it is these records that form the basis of her new book: *Victoria and Abdul* published by History Press, and a right royal read it is too.

5

A row of epic proportions

As YOU WILL no doubt know, the Ramayana, 'The Journey of Rama' is the story of one of India's favourite gods, Lord Rama, and includes his mission to rescue his wife Sita who has been captured and imprisoned by Ravana, the ten-headed demon-king of Lanka. Along with the Mahabharata, it is one of India's two great national epics, and for centuries the 25,000 verses of this Sanskrit poem presenting a highly floriated portrait of Rama as the embodiment of justice, righteousness and nobility, have brought solace, inspiration and a sense of national cohesion to Hindus. Both these tales, which the West and the westernized would call mythology (i.e. imaginative and not really 'real'), are taken as history by the vast majority of Indians; the Sanskrit word for epic is *itihasa* which means 'thus it happened'. So the orthodox accept without question that Rama lived 'five thousand years ago', which is shorthand for some unspecified time in the far distant past, they believe that the events recounted in the Ramayana and Mahabharata actually happened and happened in the way recounted. To accommodate such conflicting perspectives we need a capacious concept, so let us coin what one lover of India, the artist, versifier and prolific neologist Edward Lear, called a 'portmanteau word'. Let us speak of 'mythistory'.

That the Ramayana still grips the Indian psyche is abundantly clear. Millions read the stories daily in comic book form, and whatever your age, these *Amar Chitra Katha* publications are an enjoyable and painless shortcut to boning up on the hugely complex world of Indian mythistory. Then there was the television series in the mid-1980s; to call it a hit would be a massive understatement. The entire country virtually closed down each Sunday morning for over a year while the saga was showing. Shops pulled down their shutters, streets were deserted, people would bathe and do *puja* to their TV sets before the week's episode began. One particular Sunday I was in Allahabad when the local transmitting station broke down due to power shortages. It was attacked and ransacked by a mob furious at having been deprived of its dose of spiritual sustenance.

The only dissenters from this rather cosy picture have been the academics, always a rather contrary lot. They have pointed out that there are several versions of the epic and it is full of dubious and not even very subtle interpolations. Sanskrit was the language of the *brahmins*, they say, and so the text is not only unrepresentative of the people at large, but is also full of special pleading on behalf of that priestly elite. There is even a theory that Rama's journey is actually a reworking of an ancient *jataka* (one of the stories of the previous incarnations of the Buddha) and not a stellar example of Hinduism's creative originality at all. In short, according to some scholars, the Ramayana has been used over the centuries as a piece of propaganda for a particular world-view of the ruling elite caste, and one which places that group squarely at the centre of the universe.

What we are seeing here is the familiar debate between the believer who unquestioningly takes a mythistory at its face value as a unified and quasi-divine whole, and the academic who picks the text apart and reveals it to be a patchwork of all too human origin. Exactly the same thing happens with the Bible. All this would remain a storm in a scholarly *chai* cup had it not become part of a wider battle that has been raging in the worldwide intellectual community since the 1980's. The fight is over who has the right to tell a country's history. The buzz-word here is 'narrative'; which narrative (i.e. version of events) is correct? Who should decide? Assorted groups — racial minorities, feminists, left-wingers — argue that their experience has never been adequately represented in the national chronicle; history, they say is 'his story' and it is always told by the winner. The relevance of this debate, as lively in the UK as it now is in India, is not just confined to the sheltered halls of academe. A country's view of its own history inevitably impacts on its sense of national identity, its definitions of citizenship and the legacy it wishes to bequeath to the next generation. Whoever controls the past controls the present and thereby the future. So as everyone wants to control the present, 'narrative' is an important affair.

Nowhere more so than in India, where recent events have redrawn the battle lines more sharply. It all began innocently enough with an essay penned by the late scholar AK Ramanujan for a University of Pittsburgh conference in 1987. The essay was called: *Three Hundred Ramayanas: Five Examples and Three Thoughts on Translation*. Ramanujan's aim was to draw attention to what he called the 'simply astonishing' number of versions of the epic which have existed in India and elsewhere for the past 2,500 years or more. Not only are there twenty-five renditions of the epic in various genres — poems, stories, homilies — in Sanskrit alone, there is the *Ramcharitmanas*, a version composed by Tulsidas, a contemporary of Shakespeare, in his local dialect of Hindi called Awadhi. This vulgate version has always been hugely popular. In fact, at least 22 languages including Chinese, Laotian, Thai and Tibetan have their own versions, and many of these languages have more than one telling of the epic. And then there is the huge expanse of south-east Asia, with all those masked plays, puppet shows and shadow dramas that enact Ramayana stories. All in all, one is forced to concede Ramanujan's point: three hundred Ramayanas and then some.

So millions of people clearly love the Ramayana in all its various forms, fine, what is the problem? The problem is the Hindu right-wing. This is a very broad church, whose strongest political expression is the Bharatiya Janata Party (BJP). But it also embraces cultural organisations such as the Vishva Hindu Parishad (VHP) and quasi-military cadres like the Rashtriya Swayamsevak Sangha (RSS) — one of whose members assassinated Gandhi for being too tolerant. Then at street level there are assorted thugs and rabble-rousers, most importantly Shiv Sena ('Shiva's Army') particularly strong in Mumbai, where it likes to harass Muslims and immigrants to the city who don't speak the local Marathi language and Bajrang Dal ('Hanuman's Boys') who seem to have something against the letter 'c' — their *bêtes noires* include cow-slaughter, communism and conversions to Christianity. It must be added that this rather motley rightist collection also has on its fringes millions of Hindus both in India and around the world who are not at all fanatical or chauvinistic, just keen to preserve their faith and a sense of national identity in the midst of secular modernity.

The heart of the Hindu right is committed to the concept of *Hindutva* ('Hindu-ness') as the one thing that can unite India's majority. *Hindutva* is a bulwark against assorted threats: Islamic jihadism, globalisation, the cultural and financial imperialism of America and the secular, individualised liberalism that is modern life. To the right wing, being a good Indian means being a good Hindu, and being a good Hindu means, among other things, subscribing to the national mythistory you were taught as a child, central to which is that epitome of virtue and rectitude, Lord Rama, as national hero. To the right, history is properly seen not as an account of the endless vicissitudes of human society, but as an education in fundamental and eternal principles of morality and behaviour. To question the genesis of mythistorical texts or to suggest that they are culturally relative rather than divinely absolute, is not conducive to the establishment of *Hindutva*. Ergo, the work of scholars like Ramanujan is not in the national interest and so should not be tolerated.

The first protests against the inclusion of *Three Hundred Ramayanas* in Delhi University's syllabus came in 2008. Delhi's academics stuck to their guns and refused to drop the essay, though the head of the history department did get beaten up by some goons. Then, three years and more pressure later, the University Vice Chancellor overruled his own committee and decided to remove the offending book from undergraduate reading lists.

The row then spread to Ramanujan's publishers, the venerable Oxford University Press (India), as militant Hindus got this most respected of academic houses to stop publishing and selling the collection that contained the essay. They even secured a court apology for any offense that may have been caused. This in turn prompted 450 scholars to sign an irate letter to OUP's chief executive in the UK, expressing their 'shock and dismay' at the company's craven policy in the face of such illiberal intimidation. What about academic freedom, the exchange of ideas, free speech? The letter drew some big hitters from the small world of Indology, including Sheldon Pollock, the Professor of Sanskrit & Indian studies at Columbia University, Wendy Donniger a renowned academic from Chicago and several authors who have published with OUP over the years. The letter called for OUP to withdraw its court apology, publicly state that it is committed to the right of scholars to publish their work without fear of suppression or censorship, and demonstrate this commitment by reprinting Ramanujan's collection. If they were unable to show this much 'courage in the face of fanaticism' they must relinquish all rights to Ramanujan's work. OUP replied that they welcomed dialogue, but added that the decision was taken on 'standard commercial' reasons because not enough people were buying the book. The only pressure they had bowed to was that coming from those unemotional men in the company's accountants department.

Unsurprisingly, students in OUP's home town took up the cause; the city of dreaming spires was abuzz with demands for the right of unfettered academic opinion and the free exchange of ideas. The topic of 'non-state censorship' was debated in the Union.

Anyway, eventually the smoke cleared. Shamed by the international outcry, OUP backtracked and agreed to republish not only the collection of Ramanujan's essays that contained *Three Hundred Ramayanas*, but a couple of other books on the subject of Ramayana variations into the bargain. Result: a three for the price of one deal, available immediately at all good bookshops across India and, of course, on the web. The publishers also deny ever having apologised in court, saying that such reports were a 'misinterpretation'. The academics, for their part, are mollified, expressing a 'deep satisfaction'. It will be interesting to see if the sales of all these reprints actually reflect the interest the affair has generated; I somehow doubt they will.

Nevertheless, the episode gains a greater importance perhaps, when recognised to be but the latest in a succession of incidents that began in earnest in 1988 with Salman Rushdie's *Satanic Verses*, a book still banned in India today. A couple of years ago Mumbai University withdrew from its curriculum a Booker short-listed novel by Rohan Mistry after Shiv Sena demonstrations against its 'derogatory' references to party members. Mr Mistry said the move was "a sorry spectacle of book-burning". Then the state of Gujarat banned Pulitzer Prize-winning Joseph Lelyveld's *Great Soul: Mahatma Gandhi and his struggle with India* long before it had been released in India. The state's ruling Hindu nationalist politicians had been told that the book sensationalised Gandhi's friendship with a German man, who may have been homosexual. All this was far from true, but the ban stayed.

Most shocking to the world intellectual community was the case of another Muslim, M.F. Husain, widely acknowledged to be India's greatest living artist, a flamboyant and rather Dali-esque iconoclast whose subjects included the British Raj and Gandhi as well as episodes from the Mahabharata and the Ramayana. It was his depictions of Hindu goddesses, sometimes in suggestive poses, that earned him the long-running ire of the Hindu right. He was taken to court as a pornographer and blasphemer; when that failed militants attacked his house and vandalised paintings there. In 2006, he was charged with 'hurting the sentiments of people' because of his portraits of Hindu deities naked, and there were numerous death-threats. At the age of 92, he had been nominated in Kerala for the state's supreme cultural award but in the face of protests the high court there suspended his prize. Eventually a disillusioned Husain left India for good, adopted Qatari nationality and lived in self-exile in London and Doha, where he died in 2011.

And now, in early 2012 and a quarter of a century after its publication, the echoes of *Satanic Verses* reverberated yet again when Indian Muslim groups protested against Salman Rushdie's inclusion as a speaker at the internationally prestigious Jaipur Literary Festival. The author eventually cancelled his appearance when news circulated that three armed hitmen had been despatched by the Mumbai mafia with orders to assassinate him. But, smoke and mirrors — the rumour then spread that the *fatwa* assassins were a ruse cooked up by politicians and spread by the Rajasthani police to placate local Muslims in the run up to the imminent elections in which the Muslim vote was crucial to the ruling government. In the event, even a Rushdie video presence was called off by the organizers who feared protesting groups would barge in on the festival. Confusion worse confounded. Not long after this fiasco, Pakistani cricketer-turned-politician Imran Khan refused to participate as keynote speaker in the India Today symposium in Delhi, where the author of *Satanic Verses* was also scheduled to speak, saying 'he could not even think of participating in any programme that included Rushdie who has caused immeasurable hurt to Muslims across the globe'.

Attacks on freedom of expression — or defenses of India's cultural integrity if that is how you see them — occasionally extend well beyond her shores. In London some years ago a man attending a lecture by the aforementioned Chicago academic Wendy Doniger, well-known in the trade for her lusty Freudian perspectives on Indian mythology, threw an egg at her, incensed 'by the sexual thrust of her paper on one of our most sacred epics'. Three years later protests against an exhibition down the road in the prestigious Asia House gallery culminated in the aforementioned Husain's paintings being sprayed with black paint and the forced closure of the show. In New York a 2011 screening of *Sita Sings the Blues*, a quirky and award-winning take on the epic by Jewish-American animator Nina Paley, was cancelled after a local Hindu group bombarded the organisers with hundreds of protest emails.

An even stranger but related story comes from Spain. Three Burger King outlets there used an image of Lakshmi, the goddess of wealth, in promotional posters. Several Hindu groups in America objected by writing to the chain and protesting on the Internet. They stressed, among other things, that Lakshmi's image should not be used to sell hamburgers because most Hindus are vegetarians. Right on cue, a group of Hindus succeeded in getting their case admitted in the New Jersey Appellate Court after *samosas* that they had ordered at a diner turned out to contain meat, even though they had explicitly ordered vegetarian ones. They want the diner to pay for their pilgrimage to the north Indian town of Haridwar, so they can take a dip in the holy River Ganga and wash away their sins. The case is continuing.

The potential problems posed by freedom of speech in our electronic and multicultural age are horrendously complex, but we do seem to be witnessing the emergence of a kind of competitive intolerance. Hindus, after realising that other faiths are able to attract attention by challenging text, interpretations, films, books, music and imagery, are indulging in identity politics in a way that is quite new for what has long been regarded as one of the world's most tolerant religions. Critics of *Hindutva* politics lament the ease with which attacks on free expression can be mounted in a country which never tires of calling itself the world's largest democracy. They say this betrays a weak and ineffectual government which, while it is prepared to engage in legal action against Google to get it to clean up the level of what it beams into the subcontinent, often fails to respect and protect those who dissent from the mainstream. On the other hand, the land of Lord Rama has an ancient, nourishing and venerable culture that surely has every right to continue as it wishes. But who will decide the form it takes? Will India's Sita-soul be captured by the bombastic Ravanna-demon of secular modernity and fall foul of its many-headed cultural pluralism? The hallmark of a genuine epic is that it can be reinterpreted for each new generation; India's Ramayana looks set for a dramatic modern re-telling, and one that is surely going to run and run.

6

Belated recognition for a Sufi spy

IN SEPTEMBER 1944 a young and beautiful British agent code-named Madeleine was executed by the Nazis in Dachau. For several months she had been the sole spy operating in the highly dangerous milieu of occupied Paris. Despite ten months of imprisonment and torture by the Gestapo, she revealed nothing and her last act was a defiant shout of: 'Liberty!' What makes Madeleine's story all the more remarkable is that her real name was Noor Inayat Khan, she was the daughter of an aristocratic Sufi mystic and musician, and before the War she had devoted herself wholeheartedly to working for India's independence from the British Raj.

Noor joined the Special Operations Excecutive, set up by Winston Churchill at the low point of the war when the whole continent of Europe was under Nazi domination. Its battle cry was to 'set Europe ablaze' — more informally its agents were told to 'make a bloody nuisance of themselves'. Their means included sabotage and assassination but more routinely, liaising with Resistance groups. Noor was sent as the first female wireless operator to France, a combat theatre where life expectancy was a mere six weeks. Until as late as 1943, SOE agents received little support from a French population that feared German reprisals and the security lapses of the incompetent London team handling them from its Baker Street headquarters was shocking. Nevertheless a stream of brave women kept coming to fight for the allied cause. One of every four SOE's female agents was killed in action, many of them in Nazi camps: Andree Borrel, Vera Leigh and Diane Rowden in Natzweiler; Yvonne Rudellat in Belsen; Elaine Plewman and Yolande Beekman in Dacchau. Violette Szabo, who was posthumously awarded the George Cross, died in Ravensbruck.

Some of the SOE women were larger than life personalities. Most famous was Nancy Wake (said to be the model for the heroine Charlotte Gray in Sebastian Faulks' eponymous novel), a hard-drinking, foul-mouthed Kiwi whose passions were gin, sten guns and generally roughing it. Princess Noor could hardly have been more different. Refined and diffident, she was recruited even though she confessed to her handlers that she could never tell a lie. On a training exercise in Hampshire she was stopped by a policeman who asked her why she had a wireless set in her bicycle basket. "Because I'm training to be a spy" was the disarming reply.

The Sufi princess was sent to Paris anyway and joined the Prosper circuit, already deeply compromised as it had been betrayed by a double agent. She ran a cell of informers there, frequently changing her name and appearance, until betrayed herself at the age of 30 by the jealous girlfriend of a comrade. Tortured by the Gestapo in their notorious Avenue Foch headquarters, she managed to escape but was then recaptured and re-interrogated. After the War the head of the Gestapo, Hans Kieffer, was quoted as saying he could get nothing out of her.

Born in Moscow to an American mother who hailed from New Mexico and was related to Mary Baker Eddy, the founder of the Christian Science movement, Noor was educated in Paris and carried the British passport of an imperial subject. This was some irony, as she was also the great-great-great-granddaughter of Tipu Sultan, the 'Tiger of Mysore' who fought so ferociously against the British before being eventually killed in battle in 1799. It may have been family tales of his bravery that led her to carry a pistol through the streets of Paris, but such behaviour was not forecast by her early life. She studied psychology at the Sorbonne before becoming a childrens' writer, and like her father, a devotee of Sufism, the non-violent and mystical heart of Islam. His collected works: *The Sufi Message of Hazrat Inayat Khan* remain one of the best accounts of the subject. After the War, her brother, Vilayat Khan, became head of the Chistis, a Sufi order founded by the guru of the Mughal emperor Akbar the Great. For many years he led the International Sufi Movement, presenting traditional Eastern spiritual practices to modern Western understanding.

Before the War both Noor and Vilayat were working for the Indian independence movement; their father was close to Gandhi. But when conflict broke out in 1939, they immediately travelled to London to join what they saw as the greater cause of fighting Nazism. Vilayat went into Naval intelligence, but while Noor was initially rejected for the Womens' Auxiliary Airforce, her quiet dedication, fluent French and skill as a radio transmitter eventually marked her out for the SOE.

Honoured in France, this Anglo-Indian heroine was until recently quite forgotten in Britain, but that has begun to change. A campaign was launched on New Year's Day 2011, the 96th anniversary of her birth, to raise £100,000 to install a bronze bust of her in Gordon Square, central

23

London. It was here in the heart of Bloomsbury that she lived as a child and where she returned to while training for the SOE. Princess Noor's memorial would be the first raised to a Muslim or female Asian in Britain and the campaign is backed by 35 MP's and many others in the public eye. A £10 million bio-pic is also in the offing.

Although her superiors were slow to recognize her talents, once posted to France, 'Madeleine's' extraordinary courage and ability became clear, distinguishing her short life as a strange and rather poignant tale of various patriotisms, genuine spirituality and courageous service to a worthy cause.

7

Big fat Indian weddings

WESTERNERS are often gobsmacked at the size and scale of Indian weddings. Not long ago, a man returned from Dubai to be married up the road from here. He invited 10,000 guests, and those who came from any distance, and most did, had their petrol paid. But that is peanuts compared to the extravaganzas the beneficiaries of the New India are mounting these days.

A wedding begins with the invitation of course, and nowadays it is no longer enough to have a top designer create an exclusive little number for you. To be that little bit special, invites should come in outlandishly fashioned goodie boxes, accompanied by 'his 'n her' designer watches, Belgian chocolates, rare cognacs and if travel is involved, business-class air tickets. This last is increasingly important as multiple destination weddings become the rage. In India itself, Goa with its beaches is still a big destination and so is perennially romantic Rajasthan; last year the wedding of a billionaire jeweller's daughter booked all several hundred rooms in the five big hotels in Jodhpur and a local one-day cricket match was arranged as part of the entertainment.

But the party is moving further afield. Nuptials were recently celebrated over several days at various grand villas rented around Florence, ending up at Ferragamo's famed castle. In the exotic location stakes Thailand, the Maldives, and Dubai are current favourites — especially Thailand because you can hire a whole island. But hey, why stop there when you can hire a whole country? Lichtenstein is apparently up for grabs at half a million pounds. The host of such a moveable bash travels like a latter-day Mughal with his entourage. For a wedding held in London not long ago the host filled one chartered plane with guests and a second to carry photographers, event managers, the set designer and his staff, the entire culinary team and also his own family servants.

Many weddings are themed. India's IT capital Bangalore prefers Moroccan and Arabic sets at the moment, while elsewhere Phantom of the Opera seems to be much in demand. Rajput forts, Hindu temples, spice markets, whole cities — whatever you wish can be re-created at the flick of a designer's magic wand.

The entertainment is of course a major feature of any wedding. While Chennai still prefers Indian musicians and dancers and amateur family involvement on the stage, in other parts of the country international professionals are being hired in spades. Traditionalists may fancy a 100-piece orchestra from Europe or America while for the more adventurous, rap star Remez Sasson (who?) will trouser a cool $2 million for putting on a performance. Columbian singer Shakira can come and wiggle her shapely hips for half a million less. But if you are feeling hard up, or perhaps just patriotic, Bollywood A-listers are still a less expensive option; one will set you back a mere couple of hundred thousand pounds to turn up and strut their stuff for an evening.

Prisad Bidappa from Bangalore is a stellar example of a brave new breed — wedding designers who take over the entire event for their clients, oversee every aspect of it and deal with the heavy bombardment of mother-in-law flak. "Food is of course a huge item" he says. "A few months ago we shipped down seven chefs representing virtually every major international cuisine — Japanese, Chinese, Thai, Italian, Mexican, Lebanese and Spanish — along with their teams. And the menu for each day of the extravaganza has to be more exotic than the previous day's. Celebrity chefs are also flown in to be part of the act of course, but there are still a few Indian dishes that Indians can't do without". That'll be *dal* and *chapattis*, I suppose.

And then, when the gargantuan celebrations are finally over, those still able to move after stuffing down all that food are given their going-away presents. At a recent Hyderabad wedding the ladies received pearls and the men lengths of the most expensive Italian suiting. At another, guests were given digital car televisions; at yet another, iPads were the must-have souvenir.

A cross-section of the new India is indulging in the new marriage-madness: old money, entrepreneurs, industrialists, celebrities, Mumbai mafiosi. Even nouveau riche farmers are in on the act. Many of these come from affluent Punjab, which is India's bread-basket state and it is Punjabis that have the reputation for the most ostentatious splurges. Not a few of the big spenders are politicians. When Congress Party leader Kanwar Singh Tanwar's son married, the bride received two and a half million pounds pocket money plus a model helicopter made out of silver. The whole bash reportedly cost Tanwar £30 million. One might wonder where politicians get that sort of money, but this is India after all. Cue the on-off chief minister of Tamil Nadu, a corpulent creature named

Jayalalitha, who has been on trial for many months over allegations that a few years ago she blew three-quarters of the state's annual budget on the wedding of her adopted son.

India is, incorrigibly, what the anthropologists call 'a display society', i.e. if you've got it, flaunt it. The excesses described above are confined to the mega-rich but as marriage has always been by far the biggest domestic event, especially for a woman, they set a heady benchmark for everyone else in what is an ever more aspirational society. In India the union of a young couple has never been the result of their breathless infatuation and inexperienced hormones, but the very carefully thought through union of two extended families. And that union is firmly sealed not with a kiss, but with property, traditionally gold. While the glitterati may have moved beyond the yellow stuff to platinum and diamonds as their preferred nuptial bling, the average Indian is still wedded to it as the sealer on this most important of contracts. The average middle class family in Kerala, for example, now spends between £20,000 and £25,000 just on the gold that adorns a marrying daughter.

One intriguing question is whether the over-publicised commitment involved in the mega-extravaganzas will do anything to halt the growing number of divorces here. As the Indian bloodstream becomes increasingly infected with Western mores, more and more divorces are occurring, though in terms of percentage of the population, the figure is still tiny. Traditionally, divorce has never really existed in India, though in fact it was sanctioned, in the case of mutual enmity and only if both parties agree, as far back as 300 AD, in the *Arthashastra*, the most authoritative ancient text on statecraft. But in practice and for the religious, marriage was for all time, which included, if you believed in them, all future lives — a somewhat dreary prospect for those who find themselves shackled to a truly incompatible spouse.

The situation was eased by the Hindu Marriage and Divorce Act of 1955, since when changes in the general perception of a woman's role in life have further altered expectations. Widowhood was never an attractive prospect in India and much recent marriage law has been framed to protect the woman. For a long time it was impossible to get divorced if you had been married for over 20 years, but that too has now changed. It is still the case that if a man demands divorce within a year of marriage, he may well be shamed by having to serve a short custodial sentence, and depending on the circumstances, his parents may be jailed too. As divorce remains a stigma, especially for a woman, he will also have to pay a considerable sum to his ex-wife's family to compensate for the damage done to their reputation and her prospects of re-marriage.

Whether any of this would apply to those who jet off to Koh Samui for their wedding receptions is another question, and the antics of those with more dollars than cents will no doubt continue to amaze, amuse or appall us all for a long time to come. But marrying off a daughter is still the major financial headache for many, many Indians, often leading to chronic debt and sometimes worse — the rising number of suicides by hard-hit farmers is believed to be partly caused by marriage-related debt. The glittering examples of the mega-rich and their over-the-top celebrations will do nothing to ease this burden, nor the shockingly venal dowry demands of bridegroom families. In recognition of what is a growing problem, there are moves afoot by the government to limit the amount the poor can spend on their weddings by instituting a ceiling based on percentage of earnings. Whether this well-meaning attempt will prevent debt and dowry-related crimes, which at their worst have included the murder of the new bride and preventative abortion of female foetuses, remains to be seen.

8

Chilli con carnage

THE HOT NEWS is that the Indian army has cooked up a scheme to counter terrorism using the world's hottest chilli. The thumb-sized *bhut jolokia*—the name means 'ghost chilli'—is grown and eaten in India's north-eastern state of Assam. Traditionally it has been used there to cure stomach troubles as well as being a weapon used by farmers to repel marauding elephants, but now that researchers have found a way to harness the little creature's power the army's plan is to pepper terror suspects with grenades full of the stuff. And that power is awesome. 'The Ghost' was crowned the world's hottest chilli by Guinness World Records in 2007, way up there with the dreaded Moruga Scorpion and Naga Viper. All three measure more than 1,000,000 units on the Scoville scale, which, in case you didn't know, is the scientific measurement of a chilli's heat. To put these dizzying heights in their calorific context: while the humble bell pepper scores zero Scoville units and classic Tabasco sauce ranges from 2,500 to 5,000, the Mexican jalapeno chilli is about 8,000 units and cayenne pepper can, if pushed, reach up to 50,000. 'The Ghost', on the other hand, is so corrosive that laboratory chemists examining it wear protective goggles and it can burn through their latex gloves.

By the way, who on earth was Wilbur Scoville? Did he invent his scale by testing all these chillis himself? Was his middle name 'Asbestos'? Whoever he was, when word of 'The Ghost's' Guinness entry got around, gastronomic masochists the world over started offering huge sums to get their hands on the planet's fieriest. One woman made it into the record books herself after eating 51 in one sitting under the horrified gaze of Gordon Ramsay, who for once was struck expletiveless.

Anyway, India's chilli-powered grenades were declared fit for use by officials after trials at the country's Defence Research and Development Organisation. "This is definitely going to be an effective non-toxic weapon because its pungent smell can choke terrorists and force them out of their hide-outs," said project director RB Shrivastava, with a slightly sinister smile, perhaps due to indigestion. The army's decision is good news for Assam's farmers. A kilo of dried 'ghost' can sell for 1800 rupees, about £21, which is a handsome profit for the average farmer who generally survives on a subsistence level, taking home around 150 rupees (£1.75) a day. Some famous tea gardens in upper Assam are said to be keen to get in on the act. Last year it was reported that the Central Reserve Police Force — India's largest armed force, which specialises in counter-insurgency — had started using grenades loaded with the chemical pigment capsaicin to combat the stone-throwers in Shrinagar, capital of the perennially tense Kashmir region. Trials are also going on to produce ghost chilli aerosol sprays to be used by women against sexual predators ("So you fancied a hot date, did you?") and for the police to control and disperse mobs nationwide.

Is this the beginning of a whole new menu of armaments, with vegetable weapons joining chemical and biological ones in the world's bunkers? Imagine: the Biryani Blaster Bomb, the Mushroom Multi-mortar, the Gorgonzola Grenade. Defence experts or even well-known terrorists could become celebrity tv chefs in their spare time. The possibilities are endless...

Here at The Hermitage we use chillis with suitable restraint, but anytime you would like the Scoville rating of your food adjusted, just ask the dining staff. And while you are about it, why not find out from one of our cookery classes how to make the most out of those Indian spices in your own cooking? Chefs Tony and Deepak are the best of culinary guides.

Incidentally the chilli, usually considered a staple of Indian cuisine, is not indigenous to the sub-continent. It was brought by the Portuguese from South America in 16th century, putting down roots first in their colony of Goa before spreading all over the country. That it found such wide acceptance is partly due to Ayurvedic gastronomic theory, which states that hot food serves to equalize the body's internal temperature with its hot surroundings. This accounts for the fact that a nice curry and a cup of *chai* do in fact cool you down in hot weather, and that the hottest Indian food is found in Andhra Pradesh, the hottest part of the country. Now, as every old curry hand knows, even the fiercest Andhra dish can be instantly tamed into a smooth and docile ambrosia with the addition of just a few spoonfuls of yoghurt, so don't forget to try this next time you are unpleasantly surprised by that vindaloo.

Yoghurt's cooling effect raises further intriguing possibilities in the light of the army's new tactics. Could the Indian terrorist of the future go into combat smeared in yoghurt as protection against an incendiary attack of 'The Ghost'? Manufacturers could be onto a winner here, with new lines aimed at different groups: Maoist Mango, Al Quaeda Kiwi or Taliban Tooty Frooty. Enterprising free-market India could yet profit from those hot-heads who are seeking to damage her. Mmm, (maybe its time to buy shares in) Danone…

9

Curry flavours curry favour

WESTERN science is belatedly discovering a fact long known by every housewife in India — the spices traditionally used in curry have beneficial medicinal properties. One of the most benign appears to be turmeric, the bright yellow root, grown all over Kerala's hills, which gives curry its characteristic hue. Widely used as an antiseptic in the villages, turmeric contains a chemical — curcumin — that is already being tested as a treatment for arthritis and dementia, but recent lab tests by a team at the Cork Cancer Research Centre show it can destroy cancerous cells in the gullet. Medical experts said the findings published in the British Journal of Cancer could help doctors find new treatments. Dr Sharon McKenna and her team discovered that diseased cells began to digest themselves within 24 hours of being fed curcumin. With casebook scientific caution, the good doctor opined: "Scientists have known for a long time that natural compounds have the potential to treat faulty cells that have become cancerous and we suspected that curcumin might have therapeutic value." Another researcher, Dr Lesley Walker, director of information at Cancer Research UK, was a little more expansive, adding: "This is interesting research which opens up the possibility that natural chemicals found in turmeric could be developed into new treatments for oesophageal cancer, the sixth most common cancer in UK. Rates of this disease have gone up by more than a half since the 1970s and this is thought to be linked to the widely rising rates of obesity, alcohol intake and reflux conditions, so finding ways to prevent it is very important."

Turmeric may also to be a weapon against Parkinson's disease. Researchers at Michigan State University have found it prevents the clumping together of a very nasty-sounding 'slow wriggling alpha–synuclein protein' which is known to be the first step of the illness. Other research shows that curcumin attaches to cholesterol and prevents its ability to pass from the bowel to the rest of the body where it can do harm, and also helps the liver to eliminate any excess cholesterol. And not only does it reduce LDL ('bad' cholesterol) but it also acts to increase levels of HDL ('good' cholesterol). On top of that, this friendly little chap also helps keep the blood thin, thereby helping prevent blood clots and the risk of heart attack or stroke.

Another spice bringing some culinary zing into the sterile world of the laboratory is ginger. This is another root widely grown in Kerala, in fact our English name comes from the Malayalam word *inji*. Every good cook here knows that a ginger concoction taken shortly before eating improves digestion. Quaint superstition? Science has now shown that ginger stimulates the production of saliva, which in turn enlivens the taste buds and makes swallowing easier, while its constituent chemical gingerol enhances the digestive power by increasing the motility of the gastro-intestinal tract. Historically the root has always been used medicinally to calm stomach problems such as colic and indigestion, but now multiple Western studies also show it to be effective for treating the nausea caused by travel, morning sickness and even chemotherapy. Other studies suggest it may also decrease the pain of arthritis and, like turmeric, have blood-thinning and cholesterol-lowering properties applicable to heart disease. Moreover, ginger may help combat cancer. Lab studies have shown gingerols prevent skin cancer in mice and a recent study, also from Michigan, demonstrated they can swiftly dispense with ovarian cancer cells.

Several other common curry spices are being shown to have medical benefits. Too much chilli may burn your mouth but, paradoxically perhaps, it is a very effective pain killer and contains capsaicin which has been shown to be a powerful anti-inflammatory, a relaxant and an aid to digestion as well as significantly reducing the levels of sugar in the blood. Cinnamon, the sweet spice that goes so well with apple dishes, also helps the body manage cholesterol and blood sugar levels and helps improve the circulation, thereby reducing the work the heart has to do. Trials have shown it to be beneficial to those suffering with Type 2 diabetes, as well as being an aid to weight loss. As well as keeping witches and vampires at bay, pungent garlic adds spice to most folk medicine systems around the world as a powerful anti-fungal, anti-bacterial and anti-viral agent. We now know that it too is useful in acting to reduce cholesterol and lower blood pressure by its blood-thinning properties. Cumin helps digestive disorders, reduces flatulence, indigestion, diarrhoea, nausea, morning sickness, and heartburn. In Indian villages it is mixed with water and applied to boils. Last but by no means least, coriander, whose leaves end up garnishing most Indian dishes, acts as a modifier of digestive function by breaking fat down effectively and thereby preventing stomach upsets; it also seems to reduce urinary tract infections.

If all that wasn't a tasty enough prospect, news just in from Pennsylvania State University finds heavily spiced meals may do the heart good by decreasing triglycerides — "a type of fat that in elevated levels is a risk factor for heart disease," explains researcher Sheila West. Intriguingly, her study found that these decrease by about a third with use of turmeric, cloves, ginger and paprika in a meal even when that meal is itself rich in oily sauces and high in fat. This sounds deliciously like being able to have one's cake and eat it. Spicy meals also reduce insulin levels by about 20%, which is good news for diabetics, whose numbers are currently increasing rapidly throughout the West.

Back to turmeric — the very latest news is that it could be the new sniffer dog to detect hidden explosives. Eh? Well apparently, as turmeric absorbs molecules of explosive material from the air, changes in its natural light-emitting properties can be measured. This phenomenon of light sensitivity, known as 'fluorescence spectroscopy', is already employed in a wide array of sensing and analysis techniques. But it could be particularly useful in the case of explosives, many of which are hard to track down, particularly TNT, which is the ultimate needle in a haystack. As turmeric researcher Abhishek Kumar recently explained to the assembled boffins at a seminar organized by the American Physical Society: "If you have a gram of TNT, and you sample a billion air molecules from anywhere in the room, you'll find only four or five molecules of TNT — that's the reason its so hard to detect". Pretty well impossible, I'd say. Anyway, Abhishek's team at the University of Massachusetts, funded in part by the US government, is already in discussions with a company to utilize turmeric's natural absorbent qualities in a portable explosive detector device. So this tasty little yellow root, along with its fellow spices, looks like being a life-saver in many more ways than one.

10

Diamonds are a god's best friend

ANOTHER CHAPTER IN the endless saga of India's extraordinary religious life unfolds. This one involves the discovery of a temple treasure trove reckoned to be worth at least £15 billion. The hoard, which is more than the subcontinent's annual education budget, was found in Trivandrum, the capital of Kerala. It lay in six underground vaults — three of which had not been opened since 1872 — at the bottom of a deep and dangerous stairway in the Shree Padmanabhaswamy temple. This shrine has been under worship since the 8th century and, from the mid-eighteen hundreds on was the royal chapel of the rulers of Travancore, the southern part of modern Kerala.

The temple is dedicated to Lord Vishnu, the God of Preservation, and it appears he has been doing his job well. As authorities scrambled armed police to guard the shrine, local media revealed that the search team — which included religious officials, archaeologists and a representative of the current Travancore maharajah, as well as workers pumping oxygen into the chambers — uncovered a stash that included gold and silver bullion dating back to the Napoleonic era. There were also precious stones wrapped in silk bundles, over 1000 kg of gold coins, a tonne of gold trinkets and intricate pieces of jewellery studded with precious stones and a sack of diamonds from Burma mined in the days when that sorry land was British. The *piece de resistance* is a metre-tall gold statue of Vishnu encrusted with emeralds, rubies and diamonds and festooned with a bejewelled crown and an 18 foot long gold chain weighing more than 75 lbs. Most of the articles found in the temple are offerings made by devotees or belong to wealth stashed in the temple's underground vaults by the royal family in the eighteenth century. While the government appoints Shree Padmanabhaswamy's priests and scrutinises its budgets, the institution is a tax-free charity and the erstwhile royal family still controls it, unlike other temples in Kerala which effectively belong to the government. Vipin Nair, a lawyer who has been involved in the campaign to open the vaults in a bid to secure greater transparency in the running of the temple, sums it up: "This is simply unprecedented. Nothing of this enormity has been discovered in the history of independent India, so it is being discussed at the highest levels". Not just there Vipin, but in every *chai* stall all over the country. With anti-brahminism rife in modern India, many people see the find as predictable evidence of priestly corruption and want it cashed in and spent on secular projects. In Kerala, the first place in the world democratically to elect a communist government, such an opinion may be particularly strong, and in fact the Supreme Court of the land concurs. But the religious also feel strongly: a mob attacked the house of an activist who demanded the find be used for public purposes. This may have been because they felt the valuables rightly belong to Lord Vishnu and his shrine, an opinion supported by some senior politicians. "The gold was offered to the Lord" says Oomen Chandy, Kerala's chief minister, "It is the property of the temple. The government will protect the temple". Or perhaps the mob's ire was more pragmatic, stemming from the knowledge that once money falls into the hands of government officials it tends to be swallowed up by black holes far deeper and darker than any temple vault.

One unlikely beneficiary of the affair, albeit in a modest way, is Aswathy Tirunal Gauri Lakshmi Bhai, a member of the royal family and author of a work entitled *Sri Padmanabhaswamy Temple*. Since its publication in 1998, this worthy volume had patiently and without protest been gathering dust on several neglected bookshop shelves, but it has now sold over 1000 copies in a couple of months, with two reprints alone in the weeks immediately following the discovery. The publisher, one Mr. Radhakrishnan, is delighted. "It is a hot cake" he beams.

The final chapter of this extraordinary story has yet to be written, not least because one of the vaults in the temple still remains unopened. This is because over its door sits a carving of a snake. In Hindu belief the *naga* serpents are venerated as the subterranean guardians of fabulous riches, and with a *naga* lintel guarding the locked doorway, there will be a curse on the head of whoever breaks the seal. So, with bated breath, Kerala is currently awaiting its intrepid Indiana Jones to step forward.

Elsewhere in India several deities are happily ensconced on vast amounts of static wealth. Hindus believe jewels contain the subtle essence of their respective planet — gold for the sun, pearls for the moon, emeralds for Mercury — and so a hoard of jewels attracts not only material but celestial power and thereby acts to bring heavenly influences to bear down on the earth. Pious devotees and powerful royals have always donated gold and other precious objects to temples where they lie safely protected by rings of both visible fortification and invisible sanctity. Nowadays temple trusts use much of their wealth to run schools, colleges and hospitals.

Here, as so often, the sub-continent affords a living example of universal and ancient traditions that have died out elsewhere. Ever since the days of the priestly bureaucracies of Mesopotamia and ancient Egypt, the upper classes have heaped up precious objects in well-guarded depositories, to lie there, silently proclaiming the wealth, status and power of family, tribe or state. And what was formerly done in a sacred context is latterly done in a secular one: think of our museums. In America especially, priceless collections of objects are given or loaned by the wealthy to lie, sometimes unseen for years, in buildings that, like temples of old, are often surrounded by a population suffering relative poverty and deprivation. There the art loot stays, cosseted by all the trappings of a religious institution: the ceremonial unveilings for elite donors and patrons, the technical experts and recondite scholars, the coteries of privileged visitors, the endless appeals for funds and the occasional showings of the hidden treasures to the *hoi poloi*. And the most precious items reside in heavily guarded underground vaults, though nowadays it is a battery of computerised alarms and hi-tech cameras rather than carved snakes that keep their treasures safe.

In the meantime, we learn of the latest curious twist to the Kerala story. The man who initially challenged the temple to open its vaults was one T.P. Sundararajan, an ardent devotee of Lord Vishnu and the son of a legal advisor to the Travancore maharajahs. After independence, all the major temples under the control of the princely states came under the jurisdiction of local government boards, but under a special covenant, the guardianship of the Shri Padmanabhaswamy temple continued to rest with the last ruler of Travancore. After his death in 1991 a constitutional court ruled that any treaties entered into by the former royal family were now null and void. Despite this, the last maharajah's younger brother assumed administration of the temple, but there were those — and Sundarajan, a former policeman, was prominent among them — who felt that he was not the proper person for the job. Fearful for the propriety of his trusteeship and the safety of the temple's enormous stash, Sundarajan appealed to the Supreme Court for an inventory of its wealth to be prepared, hence the opening of the subterranean caverns. A month after the vaults were first opened the erstwhile cop, who had previously enjoyed excellent health, suddenly succumbed to a fever and died three days later.

Even valuing the jewels is running into problems. Such a task in a temple must by tradition be undertaken by five *brahmin* males. However, the state gemology department has only three experts on its books, and of these two are automatically disbarred as one is a woman and the other a Christian. The third expert, who is at least a Hindu, is currently 'engaged elsewhere' on departmental business. Retired government gemologists are being sought out.

Its spectacular hoard may well establish Shree Padhmabhavana as the richest temple in India, a position long held by another shrine dedicated to Vishnu, the Venkateshvara temple of Thirupati in southern Andhra Pradesh. Here the deity, popularly known as Shree Balaji, presides over coffers said to hold gold and jewels worth well over £7 billion. His temple is the most visited place of worship in the world. With the average daily number of pilgrims at almost 100,000 and the major festivals regularly drawing half a million a day, the annual total is about 40 million people — the entire population of Argentina. Thirupati's collections yield £3 million *per diem*, with gold, the preferred donation, piling up 3000 kgs each year. As a sideline, the god is also present as a non-executive director of dozens of prominent and successful local businesses, officially named as a member of the board.

But its not just the cash — everything at Thirupati is on a mind-boggling scale. At the annual Pushpa Yagam festival, which aims to avert natural calamities such as floods, epidemics and earthquakes, no less than seven tons of brightly coloured and sweet smelling flowers are offered to the deity.

Shree Balaji is believed to be a particularly merciful form of Vishnu who fulfills a devotee's every wish and so he is particularly popular in the Kali Yuga, the Dark Age of Ignorance through which, according to Hindu belief, humanity is currently living. But apparently even such great deities are not immune to the crippling cost of getting married in India. To pay for his wedding, Shree Balaji was forced to borrow 11,400,000 gold coins from Kubera, the notoriously exacting god of wealth. It is to help pay off this loan that devotees endure queues of up to eight hours to pour funds into the temple's coffers. Many of them also offer their hair — over a ton piles up each day — which is auctioned off several times a year to international buyers for use in wigs, hair extensions and cosmetics. This custom, which nets the temple treasury another £4 million annually, is said by tradition to date from an altercation with a shepherd (or perhaps a shearer) in which the Lord lost a small portion of his flowing locks.

To balance what outsiders may see as the all too venal side of popular religion, another very different aspect of Lord Venkateshvara resides further west at the 1,500 year old Shree Balaji temple outside Hyderabad. This particular deity is admirably immune to material blandishments, for his is the only temple in India that does not accept any money, has no collection boxes and no 'green channel' or special privileges for visiting VIPs and VVIP's to jump those enormous queues. This shrine also fought and won the right to stay out of government control. Balaji is popularly known as 'Visa God' as he specialises in granting visas to travel to the West, especially America. So, albeit in a mundane and Kali Yuga sort of way, at least this deity can be said to fulfill his role as one who transports his devotees to the other side...

11

Even the good times can go bad

Times are tough for India's most flamboyant entrepreneur, the high-flying Vijay Mallya. Something of a force of nature and the embodiment of the new free-market India shaking off the rusty shackles of government regulation and Soviet-inspired central control, Mallya is best known for his Kingfisher airline catchphrase 'Fly the good times'. But his meteoric rise began with another type of high. When Mallya's father died in 1983, the young Vijay, not yet thirty, took over his United Breweries Group and began a dazzling business career as a liquor baron. Among his best known early deals was the acquisition of Whyte and Mackay, the famous Scottish liquor company; today his United Spirits is the world's second largest booze maker, controlling three-quarters of the Indian market. Then there is his Kingfisher beer, which has far outflown other avian beer brands such as Eagle and Rosy Pelican: of each bottle downed in the subcontinent, half comes courtesy of Vijay Mallya.

The young man from Bangalore went on to buy newspapers, fashion and movie magazines and a TV company. In time he added Indian cricket and football teams to his portfolio, and along with Bernie Ecclestone and Britain's richest man Lakshmi Mittal, was recently part of the consortium that acquired West London's Queens Park Rangers football club. He likes motor racing too; he owns a racing team and has been the driving force in getting Formula One into India. As a businessman, Mallya publically disdained politics for years, at least until he decided to fund a party and become an MP in the upper house.

The man is something of a cross between Richard Branson and Silvio Berlusconi, combining the puppy-like energy of the former with the snake-oil gloss of the latter. While naming his racing team Force India may or may not have been in emulation of Berlusconi's slogan 'Forza Italia!' Mallya certainly shares the Italian's love of lavish parties, which he throws at his skyscraper home in Bangalore, his palatial villa in Goa and on his yacht, the Indian Empress. So far there have been no bunga bunga scandals, though his libidinous reputation and the video that welcomes passengers on board Kingfisher with a smiling "All our flight attendants are personally chosen by me" do little to dispel rumours of the mile-high casting couch used to recruit those micro-skirted scarlet hostesses. Funnily enough, Mallya's current woes coincide with the fall of the old Lothario who has done so much to educate young women in the inner workings of Italian politics.

On the other hand, at the moment the Kingfisher man looks far from becoming the subcontinent's Branson. As the boss of Virgin Atlantic floats his new Upper Class suite at £6,000 for a London–New York return, where one will be pampered by a cabin crew who have been trained to calm their passengers by speaking to them in whispers, and airy plans are afoot for Virgin Galactic to offer commercial space trips in 2013, back down here on planet earth Vijay Mallya is fighting for his life.

It was when he mixed drinking and flying that things started to go wrong. Kingfisher airlines hasn't turned a profit in the nine years since its founding and today its debts total almost £1000 million, with losses of some £60 million posted in the last quarter of 2011. The money for fuel, salaries and landing dues is running out; bank accounts have been frozen by income tax and excise authorities; the Indian Airport Authority is demanding weekly settlement of money owed if Kingfisher planes are to be allowed to continue using its facilities and oil companies are doing the same for providing fuel. Then, in March 2012, with the story featuring daily in India's media, Kingfisher was suspended from the international IATA organization, making it difficult for travel agents abroad to sell its tickets.

Though the tycoon could well bail out the company from his own assets he not unreasonably blames the company's woes on central and state governments for confining too many of his fleet to unprofitable routes and for changing regulatory goalposts by imposing punitive extra taxes with no warning. He is right, Indian governments of all hues love sudden and draconian price hikes. Fuel costs have also soared with no regard for the general business climate; in India they account for about 40% of an airline's operational cost, as against 20–25% worldwide. Kingfisher is also obliged to fly unprofitable routes as part of transport regulations that its boss complains are keeping the country in 'the bullock cart age'. Then there is the somnolent behemoth of the Reserve Bank of India, which, keeping a wary eye on the disastrous effects of Western lending sprees and also its own overheating economy, has raised interest rates thirteen times since March 2010, to the current 14%. But observers, including those who wrote a recent report for the respected Veritas Investment Research, blame Mallya himself for having sacrificed his liquor business 'on the altar of egoistic ambitions'. In other words, he disregarded the old advice that if you sail it or fly it, rent it don't buy it.

To be fair, it cannot be denied that Mallya has brought a type of glamour into what was the pretty dull world of Indian domestic aviation. His rather 1950's vision of 'the good times', which seem to consist of lots of eating and drinking while lots of pretty girls smile vacuously as they sashay leggily by, chimed well with the new optimism following the country's long overdue economic liberalization in the 1990's. For the newly-aspiring customer, many of whom had never flown before, several things made Kingfisher unique. The effusive welcome at the check-in desk, the goodie bags and very decent in-flight food, the seat-back TV screens which beam the boss welcoming passengers and inviting personal communication if you aren't happy with the service he offers (complaints receive a pretty prompt reply signed: Dr. Vijay Mallya, Member of Parliament) — all in all, Kingfisher made you feel special.

But then our man began to overreach himself. He bought another carrier, Deccan Airlines, and many say he paid too much. With Deccan he got more planes, more domestic market share and most importantly, a short-cut to the legal right to fly international routes, which the arriviste Kingfisher would otherwise have had to wait five years for. However, he also got Deccan's backlog of substantial losses. In its enthusiasm, even before the newly acquired domestic routes had been consolidated, Kingfisher began operations in the highly competitive international arena at a time when even well-established carriers were wobbling. With such a varied portfolio one would have expected Mallya to appoint hands-on CEO's reporting to him as overall chairman but in practice, apart from the alcohol businesses, he tried to run everything himself, ending up as something of an absentee landlord for his newer ventures.

The financial turmoil following the Arab Spring scuppered the airline's plans to raise further capital and it was forced to take out huge loans with a consortium of banks headed by the State Bank of India. The price was that they now hold 23 per cent equity in the company. More importantly, nine out of ten shares of the United Spirits, the crown jewel of the United Breweries group where it all began, are pledged as collateral to these institutions. Awash in liabilities but ever ebullient, Mallya is in ongoing discussions to recast the debt with a fresh consortium of 18 banks. By Spring 2012 a national debate was in full swing as to whether Kingfisher is too big to fail and if the government should bail it out. Civil Aviation Minister Ajit Singh made sympathetic noises but has ruled out a government rescue.

As the saga continues, Kingfisher's stocks are at an all time low, down over 20%, high-profile directors are quitting the board and in a bid to reduce costs the company has started closing those friendly check-in desks and curtailing both internal and international flights. Its number of daily flights has been slashed from a recently projected 400 to 150. Kingfisher Red, the budget domestic operation which did the unglamorous rounds of second-tier cities, is long gone. This closure is also a gamble though. No consumers are as price conscious as Indians — just go to any market here and watch the haggling. Scotch on the rocks has been very good for Mallya, Kingfisher on the rocks surely isn't.

On the positive side, at least the bright little bird has not dipped to the level of an outfit called Comtel, not yet anyway. While we have all grown used to budget airlines charging us for food, drinks, seat assignments and baggage, this airline's ploy of having a customer whip-round for fuel top-ups marks a new low. Hundreds of passengers on a recent Comtel charter from Amritsar to London were threatened with being stranded in the Punjab unless they each coughed up an extra £200 on top of what they had already paid for their ticket, so the airline could buy enough fuel to complete the journey. This debacle came just after the same airline had stranded 180 passengers in Austria until they could together chip in a further £20,000 to complete their flight to Birmingham. Shivering Indians were seen scouring the streets of Vienna for cash machines. Comtel, blaming travel agents, claimed to be in robust health. Since then it has cancelled all flights.

In a nice juxtaposition to Vijay Mallya's slide is the rise of Anna Hazare, which is the other item dominating the news at the moment. Hazare, the leader of a hugely popular anti-corruption campaign, is a self-confessed Gandhian, his white *khadi* clothes and Nehru cap clearly symbolizing the simple life the Mahatma advocated. Perhaps surprisingly, Mallya also has some time for the father of the nation — well, he recently paid US$1.8 million at a New York auction for the sage's meagre belongings, anyway. In fact, the two figures could hardly be further apart, and their difference starkly dramatises a growing clash of ideologies in the wider cultural context of India today: traditional sacred vs. modern secular; co-operative vs. corporate; eco vs. chemo; karma vs. pharma. The Mallya — Hazare polarity is an eery precursor of choices that this country is going to have to make more and more often as it moves into our resource-scarce, financially precarious and climatically-challenged future.

So, will the rapidly developing subcontinent learn from the West's mistakes sufficiently to avoid duplicating them? The economic journalist Edward Luce may be right when he argues, in his excellent book *In Spite of the Gods*, that the twenty-first century is India's to lose. But amidst all the optimistic India Shining ballyhoo, those with any foresight can see she is faced with some extremely difficult existential choices in managing her growth intelligently. To gandhify or to mallyarise, that is the question ...

12

From Russia with love

THE LABYRINTHINE COMPLEXITIES and elephantine pace of Indian bureaucracy are of course notorious. Taking into account a variety of factors that indicate the ease of running a private business, including government regulation and interference, the World Bank rates India 134 out of 175 economies. This is hardly news to Indians themselves, they have long bemoaned the paralysis of what is known as 'the license Raj' — a telling phrase, as it is fashionable to blame this chronic arterial sclerosis in the body politic on the legacy of the British. But what Dickens lampooned as the 'circumlocution offices' of Victorian England are by no means the whole story. For one thing, no other civilisation has produced such intricate systems of classification and convoluted regulation as its *brahmin* intellectual elite; the Indians seem to have a gene for rituals of recondite and priestly complexity. And for another, there was Russia.

After Independence Nehru, who was basically a high-minded Fabian socialist, and his Congress party, aware of India's myriad varieties and appalled by the violent sectarianism that exploded at Partition, opted to reject the American way and follow the Soviet system of a vast and hierarchical bureaucracy, able to govern with authoritarian intervention from the Centre. A series of 'five year plans' was initiated, following the model established by Stalin in 1928. When Uncle Joe died in 1953, Nehru called 'the man of steel' (which is what *stalin* means) a 'man of peace', got both houses of parliament adjourned and declared a national holiday to mourn him. The next day, embarrassment: India learned the Soviet Union had not stopped working for a minute.

At one stage, Stalin's daughter Svetlana married an Indian communist, Brajesh Singh, who had decamped to Moscow. When he died there in 1967, she came to India to consign his ashes to the Ganges, despite being warned by Premier Kosygin not to go because 'those Hindus burn their widows'. In Delhi she tried to seek asylum, but was persuaded out of it by Indian officials. She then pitched up at the American embassy demanding a visa. Again, much embarrassment, but with a crew-cut young CIA escort she got as far as Rome. Screaming about a 'CIA kidnap plot', Russia dispatched officials to detain her there, but she could not be dissuaded, and adopted the States as her home. Her life then became a somewhat unfocussed odyssey as she restlessly switched loyalties and residences between Russia and America. Eventually she settled to spend her last years in the middle of nowhere in Wisconsin, where she died in late 2011. Perhaps the bleak landscape of her last adopted home reminded her of the steppes.

In 1957, Kerala was the first place on earth democratically to elect a Communist government. Its Chief Minister, E.M.S. Namboodhripad, was a highest caste *brahmin* elected from our local town Neeleshwar. Since then the state has regularly returned various shades of red to power. At least three villages in Kerala have been (re) named Moscow, and both Lenin and Stalin are not uncommon names. One of the state's most famous film directors is Lenin Rajendran, while across the border the ex-mayor of Chennai, one of Tamil Nadu's leading leftists is M.K. Stalin. He is the son of the former chief minister of that state, though quite why anyone would chose to name their child after the world's worst mass-murderer remains a mystery. The name has not always been easy for him. When his father tried to get him into Chennai's most prestigious school, the authorities shuddered at being reminded of such a tyrant and insisted that the boy's name be changed. Undeterred, his father replied he'd rather change the school than the name, and so he did. Currently, so many Russians live in Kerala that in March 2012 they were allowed to vote in their country's presidential elections at its Honorary Consulate in Trivandrum.

The fall of the Soviet Union has done nothing to shake India's trust in Russia; the Great Bear and Sacred Cow continue to snuggle ever closer. Putin has visited five times in recent years offering information technology, telecommunications, oil, gas, mining, fertilizers. Not long ago a grateful Prime Minister Manmohan Singh described India's relations with Russia as 'a key pillar of our foreign policy'. The British Bulldog has been sniffing around too, but then just before Christmas the diminutive French Cock strutted confidently into the arena, bearing seasonal presents in its capacious beak: five nuclear reactors, umpteen Mirage fighter jets and a 10 billion euro investment plan. No mention yet of a Gallic partridge in a pear tree, and the gifts are conditional on certain sectors of the economy being 'liberalized'. The offer happened to coincide with news leaked that the Elysee Palace splurges £10,000 a day on food and drink and another £200,000 a year on flowers but whether it will entice the new India to join the *bon viveurs* is not yet clear.

Wooed, but not wowed, by such seductive advances, India is considering Sarkozy's offer demurely and at her leisure. Onwards comrades, ever onwards!

13

Girls marry frogs

PERHAPS surprisingly, the above headline does not come from a 1970's feminist tract but from a recent article in The Hindu. It announces a tale of two seven-year-old girls from a remote village in neighbouring Tamil Nadu who tied the knot with two frogs in an intriguing and ancient ritual. The young brides, Vigneswari and Masiakanni, hail from the village of Pallipudupet in Villupuram district, and the wedding took place during Pongal, the four-day harvest festival celebrated each Spring. In addition to the usual festivities of house-cleaning, the ritual cooking of new rice, drawing colourful geometric *kolam* patterns at the entrances to houses and the honouring and decoration of cows, the frog wedding was specifically conducted to prevent the outbreak of diseases in the village. As such, it belongs to a clutch of timeworn Hindu rituals known as *kanya puja* that involve honouring young girls as the embodiment of The Great Goddess and thus the symbols of potential fertility and new life.

The girls wore glittering wedding saris and gold jewellery and were spliced with their amphibian grooms in a ceremony that took place in front of the whole village. The frogs were tied to long sticks decorated with garlands, and the subsequent celebrations had all the usual elements of a traditional marriage, including a sumptuous feast. Sadly, there was no fairy-tale ending, as neither frog transformed into a handsome prince, but happily Vigneswari and Masiakanni weren't required to share even a marital kiss with their husbands. Both brides simply bid their grooms a dignified farewell before returning to their normal lives. After the ceremony the frogs were gently thrown back into the temple pond where they no doubt assumed instant celebrity status.

The custom of marrying frogs has its origins in a story in the Puranas, scriptures going back over two thousand years that are the source for countless Hindu legends, beliefs and practices. This particular tale concerns Shiva, the Lord of Transformations. Following a quarrel with his wife Parvati, Shiva, turned himself into a frog and hopped off in a sulk. Distraught, Goddess Parvati cried for days, and her divine misery caused distress and disease to spread throughout the land. When the villagers approached her to ask for help in dealing with their misfortunes, she told them to go and find the frog-Shiva and plead with him to marry a young girl; this was the only way the curse could be lifted. Parvati herself then cleverly took the form of a delightful young girl and when Shiva, well-known for his roving third eye, saw her, he fell for her charms and promptly agreed to marry her. Whereupon, both deities returned to their properly celestial forms and so were re-united. The outbreak of disease was cured, and both divines and mortals lived happily thereafter. We heartily wish the same benign fortune to Vigneswari and Masiakanni and, of course, their nameless husbands.

Married or not, frogs here in south India certainly fare much better than their cousins in the north-east. For years now the paddy fields of West Bengal and Bangladesh have been the main source of frogs for the insatiable demand of restaurants in France. At one point the export reached a staggering 500 tonnes annually. However, we meddle with nature's balance at our peril. It turned out that paddy frogs are the only predator of a certain type of beetle that devours young rice shoots, so once the fields were depleted of their natural amphibian policing, the beetles went on the rampage and massive destruction of paddy crops followed. Fortunately, according to latest reports, a balance has now been re-established between the three competing appetites — the French for frogs, the beetles for seedlings and the Indians for rice.

It should perhaps be added that The Hermitage is a place that welcomes both humans and frogs. Both species appear to enjoy sunbathing: the former by the pool, the latter by the lotus ponds. After dark they can be observed near the garden lights, where they crouch patiently immobile, waiting to catch their supper. The frogs, that is …

14

Gods go green

HINDU DEITIES ARE prone to materialise in all sorts of shapes and sizes and to make matters worse they will flaunt themselves unashamedly in all the colours of the rainbow. This polychrome promiscuity has not endeared them to some Western art critics who may put up with such pigments of the imagination from a kitsch showman like Jeff Koons, but dismiss them as inappropriately vulgar for serious spiritual art. To espouse such an ascetic aesthetic is to forget the fact that ancient Greek temples in their day were not the sober and tasteful edifices of unadorned stone we see today, but riots of colour whose original glory has been sadly dimmed by the unrelenting hand of time. Or think of the baroque exuberance of so much Roman Catholic art or the profound chromatic richness of Eastern Orthodoxy, and remember that even in unemotional England it cost more to paint and decorate a medieval church than to build it. 'Less is More' is a Protestant parsimony, and that dour religion was born as a reflection of the gloomy grey skies of northern Europe, it would never have got off the ground in the sunny south. For those whose souls have long been nourished by their places of worship providing a sumptuous feast for the senses, Luther's legacy of restraint must appear about as appetising as a diet of worms.

After all, whatever else may be in the mix, culture is always part-climate, part-geography and Hindu culture is as creatively fecund as the steamy jungles that spawned it. As in all traditional societies, its temples were the major — often only — place of celebration, colour and entertainment as well as education and religious uplift. What is so extraordinary is that in so many parts of the subcontinent they continue to be so. This differentiates India from, for example, Egypt, whose truly spectacular monuments have long been devoid of a pulsating dynamism, the faint traces of which can now be summoned only by considerable effort from the human imagination. *Deus abest.* Hindu temples on the other hand continue to be the vibrant palaces of gods and goddesses, celestial theatres constantly re-energised by priestly rites and human attention, and if their incumbent monarchs are not lauded with the appropriately unrestrained colour and ceremony, and their temples regularly given a fresh coat of paint for important festivals, we are failing in our duty as their earthly hosts. Offended, they will depart for sunnier climes and our world will rapidly go to hell in a handcart. So in Hindu art 'More is More', and incorrigibly so. Appropriately enough, the first important English book on Hinduism and its art was by a scholar called Moor. *The Hindu Pantheon* was published in 1810; the images Edward Moor brought back to his Suffolk home went on to become the seed of the British Museum's collection.

Given all this, it will come as no surprise that we now hear news of a couple of Hindu deities who have turned bright green. But fear not, dear reader, this is not the result of some unrestrained native paintbrush nor is it due to an attack of envy, nausea or bronze disease. The green in question is an impeccably tasteful shade of eco.

The first deity so to be effected is Lakshmi, the form of the Divine Mother who is worshipped as bringer of wealth and abundance. Tradition has it that each and every girl child is an incarnation of Her creative energy. A charming idea to be sure, but sadly the reality is often somewhat different. In fact, India currently has the worst record in South Asia when it comes to the sex ratio, with 914 girls for every 1000 boys under the age of six. The crippling costs of a girl's dowry are one of the factors said to account for the high rate of abortion of female foetuses. But this picture has changed dramatically in one village in the Bhagalpur district of Bihar. For every girl born in Dhahra, the villagers plant ten mango trees. The result is over 20,000 mango trees in and around the village creating what is by far the greenest stretch in the area. The male to female sex ratio is also the best in the region. Villager Nirmala Devi says, "There are two benefits of planting trees. One, we sell the fruits of the tree to make money for the girl's marriage and secondly it helps the environment".

All those mangos have certainly added to the village's prosperity, and the scheme has caught the attention of Bihar's Chief Minister, Nitish Kumar, who planted a tree in Dhahra himself and ensured a girls' school was built. Encouragingly, the message of treating a girl child as god's blessing and trees as bank deposits is spreading rapidly to other parts of a state that has long enjoyed an unenviable reputation for poverty and corruption. The birth of a girl in Dharha is now cause for well-founded celebration.

This connection between girls and trees is not a new one. Some of India's earliest sculptural remains, Buddhist *stupas* — relic mounds dating from a couple of centuries BC—depict a heavenly nymph entwining herself around a tree to symbolize nature's irrepressible fecundity. It is a theme picked up and repeated by countless Hindu temple carvings thereafter. Those familiar with more a recondite stratum of Indian folk-belief will be pleased to note how Dharar is reviving an ancient custom for modern times. This is the annual ritual, probably connected to those ancient stone carvings and still practised in remote villages today, in which a young girl, known as a *kumari*, first worships the sacred tree of the village and then strikes it with her left heel, an act which imparts her potential fecundity to the tree and thence to the community at large and its surrounding land. The girl must be pre-pubescent, as, not yet having shed even one of her awaiting eggs, she is maximally fertile. Thus does she enact her sacred and life-giving connection with the Great Goddess who nourishes all.

Lakshmi is one of the consorts of Lord Vishnu, and it is one of his many forms, Lord Venkateshwara (aka Shri Balaji), who is also going green. His gold-plated temple sits majestically in the temple town of Tirumala, surrounded by seven hills and high above lush green forests in the southern state of Andhra Pradesh. This is a place of astonishing statistics. It has an annual income of some £300 million, mostly from donations, and near about 40 million pilgrims visit to get the deity's blessings each year. Such a huge footfall puts enormous pressure on water, electricity and other energy resources. But now Tirumala is using its religious influence and economic muscle to change the way energy is used here. Developing reserve forests around the temple to act as carbon sinks, the temple management is promoting the use of sustainable technologies in a determined bid to influence public opinion in a country not renowned for its ecological awareness. LV Subramanyam is the executive officer of the temple trust. As he explains: "Most of our devotees are progressive. In a religious place like Tirumala, we can set the example by going green. Probably the impact will be much more than normal government advertisements or publicity."

The green standard bearer is the temple kitchen, a large multi-storey building open all day to do just one thing—provide free meals for pilgrims. Several cooks work in tandem stirring huge pots of rice, curry and vegetables as they prepare almost 50,000 kilos of lunch each day. On the roof above them, rows of solar dishes follow the angle of the sun and together with more solar panels on the roof of the temple itself, generate enough energy to convert water into 4,000 kgs of high-pressure steam. Reaching temperatures of 180° C, the steam cookers are fast and cheap. This holy heliotropism is both symbolically fitting — Vishnu is traditionally worshipped as an embodiment of the sun — and practically beneficial, as it saves an average of 500 litres of diesel fuel daily.

By switching to green technologies, the temple cuts its carbon emissions and earns a carbon offset, or credit, which under the Kyoto Protocol mechanism they can then sell. Badal Shaw is the managing director of Gadhia Solar Energy Systems, which has set up the solar cookers. He estimates that this one project has resulted in a cut of more than 1,350 kgs of greenhouse gases in the skies above Tirumala. "This was the first project to get a gold standard certification — it's a registered project and it is issuing carbon credits," he says. "From a monetary value, carbon being a tradable commodity — the prices keeps going up and down ... we sold the carbon credits of this and various other projects to the German government."

But it's not just the sun that the temple is tapping into. Perched on top of a hill, the site is ideal for harnessing wind energy and several companies have already donated turbines which generate a combined total of 7.5 megawatts of power. A Tirupati-based company called Green Energy Solutions now wants to develop wind farms to supply the temple's entire energy needs. Lord Venkateshvara's vast pool of devotees from the worldwide Indian diaspora is already a very generous source of donations in the traditional form of cash, jewels and gold, but now Madhu Babu, the founder of Green Energy, is looking for donations of green power. "We have found that a lot of non-resident Indians are interested in donating sustainable technology" he says "We want to facilitate such donations and translate them into wind farms, so that the entire temple town can be run on green energy."

India is growing so rapidly that the global consultancy McKinsey predicts her carbon emissions will double in the next decade. Tirumala has been identified as a future 'low-carbon footprint city' by European Aid and Development, which works under the European Commission. This is also a new educational role for the temple. In the words of one of the project officials: "When our pilgrims learn that sustainable sources of energy are being tapped into make the water, food and power available to them, it inspires them. They too will want to learn more about the technology behind it."

India is already a huge generator of carbon credits, and according to a 2010 study by HSBC Research, India's share of the $2.2 trillion market for low carbon goods and services in 2020 could be as much as $135 billion. The report further predicts that India's clean technology market is likely to grow faster than any other country's, thereby creating 10.5 million green jobs and helping to guarantee the country's energy security. This last is an important piece of the jigsaw in our uncertain political times, as the subcontinent currently spends 45% of export earnings on energy imports, and this is expected to increase even further.

Whilst Tirumala might be one small step, the hope is that this could be a model that is replicated across the country. It is also heartening to see that such progressive initiatives are being made by re-evaluating traditional cultural strengths, rather than thoughtlessly abandoning them in favour of a Western model of 'progress' that has already run into so many problems in its homelands. India's presiding deities must be relieved too. Looks like its time to get those cans of paint out again …

15

Gold's Own Country

PERHAPS Gordon Brown, Britain's late and largely unlamented Chancellor of the Exchequer, should have come and talked to some Keralites before he decided to sell off the UK gold reserves at the bottom of the market. Had he done so, he would have found that Malayalis value the yellow stuff enormously and they would doubtless have opened his bleary eyes to the fact it was going to rocket in value. But gold is not only seen as a sure-fire investment here; its possession confers huge social status and also enables people to bypass India's cumbersome and punitive banking system.

While all Indians have always appreciated the portability and easy liquidity of gold and valued it as a refuge in unstable times, nowhere in India does gold like Kerala. This may be due to her historical trading links with the wider world, her proximity to the Middle East and the gold-smuggling port of Dubai or the fact that taxes on imported gold were low until relatively recently. Whatever the reasons, the figures speak for themselves. Three states: Andhra Pradesh, Tamil Nadu and tiny Kerala account for 40% of India's annual purchase of 1000 tonnes; half of this in the form of jewellery. Kerala has over 5000 retail outlets spread throughout the state. Remittances from the Gulf and the booming price of the rubber they produce are giving some lucky Keralites spare cash, and they invest it in gold. The sleepy village of Koduvally, about twenty miles north east of Calicut, is not untypical: over 100 gold jewellery shops jostle for space within a radius of less than a mile. At the other end of the scale, in the large towns four or five big boys have air-conditioned footfall stadia selling nothing but gold. Together they spend £24 million pounds annually on advertising: open any paper, watch any tv, see the huge hoardings lining any main road. That they paid the same amount again in taxes last year (and remember that no one in India pays as much tax as they should) gives an idea of their sales volume.

Ironically, the rise in price of gold and boom in retailing is sounding the death knell for one part of the gold industry: the traditional craftsmen. Once an integral part of the community, the goldsmith learnt his skills from his father and enjoyed a close relationship with his clients, making, mending and altering their jewellery as and when needed. The specialised goldsmith caste was centred in Thrissur, Kerala's cultural capital, which until recently housed more than 10,000 artisans. Their downturn began with the liberalisation of the gold trade; the proliferation of middlemen operating between goldsmiths and jewellery shops reduced craftsman profits and the earlier skills of intricate, bespoke work have lost out to sourcing from abroad, mechanisation and bulk production. Generation Next demands new designs and even new colours — pink and white being current favourites.

Thrissur has about 3000 mechanised units producing gold jewellery for some 500 retail outlets. The workforce is composed either of traditional craftsmen who have deserted their vocation for better-paying piece work in the factory, or migrant workers. These come especially from Bengal and now account for one in four of the city's gold workers. In the last five years, Kerala's Gold and Silver Merchants Association has seen its membership drop from 7,000 to 5,000. Figures continue to fall, and with the new generation more interested in the internet than the skilled artisan's workbench, it looks as if the corner-shop jeweller will follow Kerala's tile-makers and diamond-cutters into history.

Perhaps they should go over the border to a restaurant in the IT capital Bangalore. This may be looking for staff due to its growing number of customers, which has been rocketing since the debut of their latest delicacy, a gold-plated *dosa*. This is priced at an unheard of Rs. 1,011, i.e. twenty times the usual cost of South India's favourite breakfast dish of rice flour pancake roasted crisp with a hint of oil and filled with mashed potatoes. But then this *dosa* does have a wrapping of pure gold foil.

Some of Kerala's huge demand for gold is due to the tradition of marrying off daughters weighed down by the stuff. The sales of golden tomfoolery peak in August, the start of the Malayali marriage season and a middle-class family will spend on average about £25,000 on wedding gold. This huge cost is being driven even higher by wealthy celebrities flaunting their extravagant spending in what is an increasingly aspirational society. In fact, along with the cost of illness, marriage of daughters is the prime cause of marginal families being pushed over the brink into penury.

The other reason for gold's popularity is that you can borrow cash against it; altogether India's 'gold loan' business is reckoned to be £3.5 billion annually. In Kerala, both private and state-owned 'Non-Banking Financial Companies' — pawn shops to you and me — do a roaring trade, allowing Keralites to avoid the intrusive questions, lengthy paperwork and crippling interest rates involved in getting a bank loan. Banks currently charge 18% interest,(and probably rising as you read this), whereas gold pawn shops give you cash immediately, no questions asked, at a rate of 3 or 4%. Several state-owned NBFC's have hundreds of branches throughout Kerala; even our little local town Neeleshwar has a dozen small pawn merchants. Given the continuing global financial turmoil and the current epidemic of 'quantitive easing', it looks as if these wily Malayalis have the right idea: get into that surprisingly heavy yellow stuff. Sorry Gordon, another bad decision there.

16

High-spirited bike keeps on going

IT IS OFTEN said that Hinduism has 33 million gods. Complete nonsense of course, just tourist guides' misinformation to keep their clients bemused. However, it is undeniable that Hindus do have an unrivalled genius for locating the Divine in both the extraordinary and the mundane. Nevertheless, even for those happy to see divinity in a naughty elephant-headed boy (Ganesha), a courageous and loyal monkey-general (Hanuman) and a half-man, half-lion (Narasingha, Vishnu's fourth incarnation) who likes nothing more than disemboweling demons, there is now one addition to the Hindu pantheon that may take a bit of swallowing. It's a 350cc Royal Enfield Bullet motor-cycle.

The temple enshrining this vanished pride of British engineering is to be found in Chottila, a small village in Rajasthan located on the stretch of National Highway 65 that links Jodhpur and Pali. Inevitably, several stories explain its genesis but all feature a young man called Om Singh Rathore (a good Rajput name, that), who was the son of the headman of Chottila. Om Singh had two somewhat incompatible passions: his Royal Enfield Bullet and the local alcoholic beverage. One fateful night in 1991, they combined: his vehicle struck a roadside tree and he was killed. The next day his body was recovered by the local police and they took the bike to the station as part of their investigation formalities. That night it disappeared. The next day it was found at the accident spot. The errant Bullet was brought back to the station, but the next night it vanished again, only to be found back at the fateful spot. Annoyed, the cops took the bike, emptied its fuel tank and kept the vehicle tightly bound with iron chains. That night it returned to the accident spot. Now spooked, they handed it back to Om Singh's relatives, but after villagers continued to hear it being driven round the village at night, the family hastily sold the bike on to someone in Gujarat, hundreds of kilometres away. He abandoned ownership when The Bullet vanished from his home town and turned up again in Chottila.

About this time a truck met with an accident at the same spot on the Chottila road; the driver, though injured, survived. He described how the spirit of Om Singh had appeared and saved his life by lifting him out of the mangled vehicle. That was it. To honour the spirit of its former owner, The Bullet was installed in a simple shrine whose 'deity' is parked in the open air and decorated with marigold garlands. It stands next to a platform on which there is a photo of Om Singh, also richly garlanded, and a sacred fire pit fronts the plinth. The tree that caused the fatal accident is nearby; it too is lavishly festooned with flowers, ornaments and brightly coloured threads.

Passing drivers began to slow down and blow their horn out of respect; the fame of Bullet Baba spread and people from neighbouring villages and even faraway places now come to offer prayers. No doubt there are old British bikers who would be eager to pay their leathery respects to the motorbike industry that once led the world? And while The Bullet was no Harley, perhaps Americans would also make the pilgrimage to place their iconic biking photos next to Om Singh's: Brando in 'The Wild One', McQueen in 'The Great Escape', Fonda and Hopper in 'Easy Rider'? Tour operators, take note, there is a gap in the market here.

The shrine seems especially popular with newlyweds and parents with new babies. Women donate their bangles to the tree in a time-honoured custom. Indeed, the procedure here is as in any Hindu temple: prostration, circumambulation, incense, flowers, prayers, a small financial donation, the receiving of blessed food known as *prasad*. Many devotees pour some of Om's favourite tipple into the sacred fire as an offering. The drink has been re-named 'Bullet', but whether it is this spirit that accounts for another odd phenomenon is anybody's guess. Locals swear blind that on moonless nights Om Singh's bike can still be heard roaring its way round the village ...

17

If the mountain won't come to Mahatma…

Last year a new chapter was added to that ever-expanding tome Follies of Capitalism and it was written in Indian ink with the world's swankiest pen. Montblanc Simplo, the German company that manufactures the white-tipped Mont Blanc fountain pen landed itself in trouble with its scheme to sell India a 'Limited Edition Mahatma Gandhi' line. Each pen sported an image of the great man on its trademark 24 carat gold nib and each cost 14 *lakh* rupees, which is a tad over eighteen thousand pounds sterling.

The Germans are usually renowned for their attention to detail, but someone in Simplo's market research department goofed with this particular masterpiece, and badly. To use the world's most potent symbol of frugality to market a pen costing over eighteen grand in a country where almost four out of every five people live in poverty was about as sensitive as Holiday Inn's opening a 7 star luxury hotel in downtown Calcutta and calling it The Mother Theresa.

Many Indians — who by and large have a residual reverence for the Mahatma even while frenetically aspiring to live in total contradiction to everything he stood for — were predictably furious. Nowhere more so than here in Kerala, a state which proudly remembers the important part it played in the fight for independence and its association with the Mahatma. Dijo Kappen, managing trustee of the Centre for Consumer Education, filed a petition in the Kerala High Court, charging that to make the Father of the Nation a 'symbol of a 14 lakh rupees pen is nothing but an attempt to degrade everything Gandhiji symbolised'. Montblanc immediately backtracked, promising to suspend their sales campaign until ordered otherwise by the court. They also offered an unconditional apology if the sentiments of any citizen of India had been hurt.

Whether a (white) mountain or molehill, this little story may have wider resonance. As it becomes increasingly obvious that the global financial structure is irremediably shaky, we should perhaps look afresh at the Mahatma's philosophy. While he is chiefly remembered as the wily saint of Indian freedom, his long term vision of how the planet is best placed to survive is perhaps becoming increasingly relevant to India — and the rest of the world. Sceptical? Consider three of his cardinal principles in the chilly dawning light of the 21st century. First: **sustainability**, i.e. consumption must be based on genuine need. As he pithily said "The earth provides enough to satisfy every man's need, but not every man's greed" Second: **decentralization**. Gandhiji dismissed the remote authoritarianism of the centralized state as too far removed from real people to serve them honestly or efficiently, and history has proved him right in widely varied contexts whether democratic or communist. Third: **self-respect**, i.e. developing nations should not mindlessly ape the West. Even though everyone is talking up the consumer revolutions in the new leviathan called Chindia, the simple fact is that a country's economic health can no longer be based on the developed nations' model of bulimic mass-consumerism. Such consumption of goods is clearly unsustainable in terms of resources and environmental degradation. Just consider this: if everyone on earth was to enjoy America's current average level of consumption, we would need 4 more planet earths to sustain us. Four.

Moral of the story? You can't eat a gold-nibbed pen, even if it does have a white tip like a tiny ice-cream cone. Montblanc told the court that by using the Mahatmas's image they were actually paying tribute to his 140th birthday, and to prove this a fulsome brochure praising him will be given out with each pen. Mmmm, maybe better to save the paper on that one?

18

India's brave new world?

THE THOUSAND MILE stretch of the Western *ghats*, the line of forest-blanketed hills running parallel to the southern half of India's western coast, is a cornucopia of bio-diversity and home to countless undiscovered species. This area is truly remote from modern life, no mobile phone signal here, just 5,000 types of flower, herds of wild elephants, lots of snakes and tigers. And yet an isolated valley in this primeval stretch is hoping to become one of the most advanced cities on earth.

Lavasa will be a metropolis governed mainly by machines; a central bank of computers will control everything from individual household security to transport. It will cost half a billion dollars to build and the brochures use pictures of Oxford (yes, Oxford) to illustrate how the place will eventually look. Ten years ago there was nothing here but a few tribal villagers living in low thatched huts and farming terraced hillside fields, now these people stand on the edge of a vast building site, bemusedly watching the transformation going on around them. Amidst the rubble and electricity pylons, attenuated multi-coloured apartment blocks rise in long terraces and opulent chalets nestle among the trees. But the whole place is in suspended animation as right now it's a ghost town and all of its buildings, including the state-of-the-art hospital, stand eerily deserted. Work has halted while the Indian authorities debate environmental issues surrounding the development, though few seriously doubt that the project will eventually reach completion.

Many Indian cities are almost totally unplanned, with the affluent escaping the effluent by living in gated communities protected by security guards on constant watch. Services are so bad that anyone who can afford it has their own electricity generator and water pump. When failure in the national grid deprived some 600 million people in north India of electricity for over 48 hours in the summer of 2012, the necessity of such backups became painfully obvious. The challenge for Lavasa's planners is to create a city that doesn't suffer from these problems, and the way they hope to do it is replacing fallible human bureaucrats with unimpeachable machines. Many miles from the reach of the nearest police and the emergency services, Lavasa will be forced to be its own self-sufficient entity, a digital age island-city providing its inhabitants with healthcare and education and levying its own taxes to fund them. Metre by metre, researchers are mapping the city using a geographic information system. It includes water pipes, fibre optic cables, electrical wires, transport links and the footprint of every building. If a pipe bursts in your second floor bathroom, the central screens will show exactly where it is.

Located not far from the city of Pune, formerly a large army base and now a developing IT hub only a few hours from Mumbai, Lavasa is seen as a prime real-estate development of the near future; indeed there's already a video-gaming arcade in place opposite the American diner. Soon there will be a space theme park, masterminded by the same people who created the American Space Camp in Alabama. Lavasa is India's first city designed for Generation E, a geek's paradise of e-government where every aspect of life will be online. It is estimated some 400 million Indians will migrate from country to city over the next 40 years — the equivalent population movement took a thousand years in Europe — but Lavasa's inhabitants will be capped at 300,000 to ensure its services aren't overwhelmed. So the final city will be a quarter of the size of Mumbai but with only 2% of its population.

Some fear that even this much environmental impact on this unspoiled corner will be disastrous. The work is currently at a standstill as the Maharashtra government has filed a criminal case against the developers, citing willful neglect of environmental norms as regards pollution, toxic waste, sewage disposal and contamination in the surrounding air, water and soil. Nine directors and six officials of the company have been summoned to appear in court for preliminary hearings at the end of January 2012. Alongside complaints that water needed for the city of Pune is being diverted into Lavasan swimming pools, there are also ongoing investigations into the forcible taking of land from local farmers and tribals who have lived here for centuries. When the Lavasa Corporation first arrived here 150 resident families moved out. Now their displaced members hover in groups around the edges of the development and throw rocks at any vehicle coming out of the city.

Is this really a viable vision of the future, or is Lavasa pioneering a direction that will split India even more in two by introducing a digital divide where huge economic divisions already exist? Lavasans will be living their hi-tech, sheltered lives parallel to the subsistent forest-dwelling tribes just a few kilometres away. For the scheme really to work, it would surely have to meet everyone's needs, not just those of the wealthy and privileged; this sci-fi megopolis cannot somehow be exempted from the stringent conditions that apply to the rapid growth burgeoning in the rest of the country. Against the wider background of Maoist-inspired civil unrest that is currently raging against palpable inequality in various pockets of the subcontinent, to pursue such a development equitably looks to be an order as tall as any of Lavasa's glittering and empty tower blocks.

19

India's noble pachyderm

Massive, patient, dignified, gentle but wild when roused, highly intelligent, family-minded and empathetic — of all animals, the elephant surely epitomises the Indian spirit best. And for their part Indians have always loved Kipling's 'noble pachyderm'. In Hindu mythology the saggy-baggy creatures are quasi-divine, depicted with wings, often white in colour and associated with clouds, rain and the heavenly gift of fertility. No lesser figure than Indra the king of the gods rides on one, the white Airavata, who was one of the first beings to arise out of the infinite milk ocean at the beginning of creation. He has four tusks which are sometimes depicted as trunks, a protuberance whose dexterity fascinated its early observers: the poets of the Rig Veda (c. 2000 BC) described the elephant as *mrigahastin* — 'the animal with a hand'. Fifteen hundred years later the mother of the Buddha dreamed that a white elephant bearing a white lotus in its trunk entered her side, an event the court astrologer interpreted as a sign she had conceived a great being who would become either a spiritual giant or a famous temporal leader. Fortunately, the former turned out to be the case. It is said that Lord Shiva himself moves at the pace of an elephant, and then of course there is the naughty elephant-headed Ganesh, Hinduism's favourite deity.

Some of the finest examples of the Indian artistic genius celebrate the elephant: the lovingly sculpted sandstone panels at the great Buddhist *stupas* of Sanchi and Amaravati (2nd century BC) and the oneiric frescoes in the caves of Ajanta (1st century BC) are two early examples of how the endearing character and charming foibles of the beast were unerringly captured by Indian artists. Later would come the masterly representations in Hindu temple stone-carving, later still the miniature paintings of the Mughal and southern Rajasthani schools, in which the elephant was beautifully portrayed as hunter, fighter and all round ceremonial show-stealer.

But although the Asian elephant is much gentler than its African cousin, the Indians never made the mistake of looking on it as some sort of cuddly companion, and the same is true today. Increasingly faced with declining numbers and drastic loss of their habitat, threatened elephants inhabit tiny islands of space surrounded by an encroaching sea of humanity. Naturally such pressure turns them into a potential danger. Along the Ganges, in the Rishikesh-Haridwar area alone, thirty-one people have been killed in the last five years; one beast has dispatched five villagers already this year in the adjacent foothills around Dehra Dun. Further south in the eastern state of Orissa, a herd of seventy wild tuskers has been trampling down cattle and houses, eating crops and displacing villagers for the last nine months; just last week thirty-five houses in one West Bengal village were flattened. Such things are often in the news.

Kerala is particularly fond of her elephants, which, according to a recent census, form a stable and healthy population, densest in the hill district of Wayanad. Out of the total national herd of about 28,000, some 3,500 live in Kerala's reserves and protected areas and perhaps 6,000 more roam wild in her forests. Counting these was a massive operation involving trained volunteers, forest officials and tribal trackers. The forested area was divided into a grid and in each section a tally was made by a combination of direct sightings and counting dung piles. In ancient times fresh elephant dung was also valued but for a somewhat different purpose: women would stand in it for up to an hour before engaging in conjugal rites with their husbands. Why? In order to increase their chances of conception.

These days the most spectacular display of elephants is the massive gathering of the Pooram at Thrissur, Kerala's cultural capital, each May. In an eight day event flower-garlanded images of all the local gods are borne on elephant back to gather in worship of Lord Shiva. The climax is a coming together of splendidly caparisoned beasts, each bearing a brilliantly coloured ceremonial parasol, peacock fans and yak-tail fly-whisks. They amble regally from shrine to shrine in a musical procession, somehow coping patiently with the ear-splitting firework display that, as so often in India, is the culmination of the celebrations.

Not far from Thrissur rises the magnificent Krishna temple of Guruvayur which boasts a permanent stable of over fifty elephants from all over the country, all donated by devotees as a token of piety. Here one can clearly spot the different characteristics of each regional breed — those from the hill areas like Assam, for example, have shorter legs to enable them to keep their balance in the steep terrain. Guruvayur's elephants are used mainly in the Krishna temple's festivals but they are also rented out to other shrines around the state for their celebrations.

But once the busy festival months are over, the monsoon comes and with it some well-earned rest and serious pachyderm pampering. As the tourists flee the rains and desert the Ayurvedic clinics, local elephants gleefully take their place. After months of walking on tarred roads, living on palm leaves and bananas and dignifying numerous temple functions, their routine changes each July into a month-long rejuvenation treatment. This features individual examination, relaxing massages with medicinal oil, therapeutic baths and sumptuous Ayurvedic meals that include rice mixed with ghee, wheat flour, powdered black pulses, palm sugar and various herbal powders mixed with vitamin and liver supplements. Presumably it is their unfailing memory of such lavish care that keeps the great beasts gently compliant throughout the following season.

Fortunately, we humans can have good memories too. In December 2011 the 35th anniversary of the passing of a particularly loved temple elephant, Guruvayur Kesavan, was celebrated at the shrine. A solemn procession of 24 tuskers, led by the senior member of the stable, Gajaratnam ('Jewel among Elephants') who carried a picture of the deceased, assembled in front of a statue of him. They stood with raised trunks for some time while floral tributes were laid. Kesavan was renowned for his majestic looks, intelligence and devotion to the image of the temple's presiding deity. Donated to Guruvayur by a local king in 1922, he served the temple for 54 years before passing on on *Ekadasi*, a particularly auspicious day, in 1976. Three years previously he had formally been awarded the title of *Gajarajan* 'King of Elephants'.

As befits the gravitas of his charge, the profession of mahout has always been a highly respected one. The Greek traveller Megathenese writes of the skills of this quasi-secret brotherhood. He mentions the elaborate training procedures mahouts employed, as well as how they lovingly tended to their charges and looked after them when they were ill: cow's milk was prescribed for eye diseases, pig's fat for boils and sores. A mahout had to have a keen power of discrimination to distinguish between various types of animal — those which could be trained to hunt, those suitable for work or for war. The latter were particularly important, as the horse was not indigenous to India and elephants were always the preferred beast of battle. They were trained to break down fences and the stockades and gates of forts, as well as to trample horses and infantry underfoot and charge the opposing army. All this they accomplished with great aplomb, but their one drawback was their lack of maneuverability. This became particularly evident when elephants were pitched against the horses that bore invading Muslim armies, which were very often able to run rings around their Hindu opponents. The most successful of these invasions was in the early sixteenth century with the Mughals, a family descended from Genghis Khan and Tamurlaine the Great, who came from Ferghana in Turkestan. This valley bred the swiftest of all the steppe horses; famed throughout Asia as 'the celestial steeds', they fed on fields of blue alfalfa.

The one time even a skilled mahout is powerless to control an elephant is when it is in *masth*, and Indian papers often carry reports of single beasts bolting out of temples or processions and even killing bystanders when suffering an onrush of pachyderm priapism. Usually, though, they run off for several hours, eventually get spiked by a well-aimed tranquiliser dart and all returns to normal. Ancient commentators remarked on the elephant's sexual power: two of its common Sanskrit names were *madambara*: 'the lust-garmented' and *sadadana*: 'always in rut'. Such primal energy was celebrated in traditional festivities, when elephant processions were followed by troupes of musicians, male attendants dressed in womens' clothes and hermaphrodites in bizarre costumes, while the spectators shouted bawdy remarks as the procession passed by. The whole event — which sounds similar to Western carnivals celebrating the Lord of Misrule — was believed to bring rain and ensure fertility for the coming year. Sadly, this custom died out in the 1850's, perhaps under the weight of the Raj's disapproval.

If so, the Brits are certainly making up for spoiling the show. Elephant Family, a charity founded by Mark Shand, conservationist and author of the delightful *Travels on my Elephant*, does fine work as the UK's biggest funder for the endangered Asian elephant, whose numbers have plummeted by 80% in the past 100 years. It works to set up 'elephant corridors' as safe areas for the wild herds, and here in Kerala over 700 tame beasts are currently micro-chipped as part of the charity's scheme to assemble an accurate database.

Elephant Family's latest international project is Elephant Parades in many major cities worldwide. Up to 250 large models of the beast made by well-known artists are exhibited around the city before being auctioned. The Parade that took place in London in 2010 raised £4 million. As part of the event, a consignment of elephant dung large enough to fertilise the average suburban garden for a year was auctioned off in Richmond, West London's desirably leafy suburb. This gathering of the great and the good was presided over by the Prince of Wales and the Duchess of Cornwall, (who is Shand's elder sister) and Britain's Asian business elite was well represented: steel billionaire Lakshmi Mittal and the millionaire king of the ready-made curry, Sir Gulam Noon, were among those attending. The dung had been generously donated by three Indian elephants belonging to Lord Robin Russell, a trustee of the charity, and the chairman of Sotheby's conducted the sale. All in all, it was a suitably grand event in aid of the worthy cause of supporting the noblest of creatures.

20

In the future, the eyes will have it

DESPITE being named after the Hindu goddess of wealth, Laxmi earns only about £1 a day, sorting cast-off clothing for recycling. She has only one name, as do many of India's poor, but she couldn't read it if it was written down for her, and though she thinks she's 30 she's not exactly sure as she has no birth certificate. In fact, Laxmi has no official ID of any kind for that matter: no driver's license, no voting card, no social security number — nothing at all to document her existence. But she does have a pair of large, brown and rather beautiful eyes, and they have just been captured on a computer screen and transferred to a data base. From this moment on, Laxmi is the rather bemused owner of an official existence, for she has just become part of what is by far the biggest and most technologically complicated biometrics programme ever attempted.

Laxmi and her two children are the latest among millions of people enrolling in India's Unique Identification Project, known for short as Aadhaar, which means 'Foundation' in several Indian languages. Its mind-boggling goal is to issue identification numbers linked to the fingerprints and iris scans of every single member of the population — which currently totals 1.2 billion and rises each year by 40 million, the total population of Argentina.

If successful, the Aadhaar identification number will serve as a verifiable, portable and all but unfakeable national ID. Previous registration schemes have always bitten the dust, so this time the government approached the 'Bill Gates of Bangalore', billionaire Nandan Nilekani, to get the job done. Nilekani co-founded the outsourcing giant Infosys in 1981, building it from a seven-man office into a leviathan employing more than 130,000 people. Then he turned his attention to projects in the public sector, working on government schemes to improve welfare services and e-governance and was named by Time magazine as 'One of the world's 100 most influential people'. It is Nilekani's reputation that is giving Aadhaar's supporters the confidence that it will succeed as a pivot the Indian government's campaign for financial inclusion. Today, there are as many as 400 million Indians who, like Lakshmi, have no official ID of any kind. And if you can't prove who you are, you're pretty much locked out of the formal economy, unable to access government programmes or get a bank account, a loan or insurance.

That today less than half of Indian households have a bank account is also due to a long-time and deep-seated mistrust of banks; when in need people rely on local money-lenders and when in surplus they stash cash under the mattress. So the timing of Aardhaar is rather counter-intuitive: Indians are being persuaded to get the banking habit at precisely the moment most of the rest of the world is bitterly ruing their misplaced trust in what they are belatedly realising to be greedy, reckless and incompetent institutions. The other way Indians traditionally save is by putting their money into easily transportable and exchangeable gold, and in the present global crisis — as in all crises — guns and gold are more than ever the smart investments. We will come to the guns in a moment, but Indians are certainly buying the yellow stuff as the price continues to climb, and using it as surety against loans is becoming a popular way of raising cash. Even the conservative Reserve Bank of India is steadily adding to its existing hoard of 550 tonnes; in the past couple of years it has added almost £13 billion to its gold reserves.

The advantage of money in a bank, in theory anyway, is that it can gain interest, and while each of India's poor may have only a tiny amount to save, there are hundreds of millions of them. A deposit of just Rs. 350 (c. £5) per head would add billions in new capital to the financial system. And once banks have more capital they could be lending more and less punitively. As it is, getting a bank loan in India is, for all but the mega-rich, like squeezing blood out of a stone; months of paper-work circulated around assorted circumlocution offices ends up with the prospect of an interest rate that has risen twelve times in the last eighteen months. Currently it is an eye-watering 18 per cent.

Nilekani has recruited high-flying Indian IT techies from around the world, and to date Aadhaar has far outpaced the elephantine slowness of typical governmental schemes. Launched in September 2010, his project has already enrolled 16 million people and the pace is accelerating. It takes only 10 minutes to enter someone into the database; by the end of 2011, the agency expects to be signing up 1 million people a day. Using both fingerprints and eyes makes the task considerably more complex, but although iris-scanning is not perfect, at least it bypasses the problem of trying to fingerprint the millions of adults whose pads have been worn smooth by long years of manual labour and the millions of children under 16 whose fingerprints are still developing.

Quite apart from the challenge of reaching villagers who have never seen a computer, persuading them to have their irises scanned, ensuring that their details are accurate and safeguarding the resulting mountains of information, the sheer amount of data will make it extraordinarily difficult to manage. Each record must be matched to only one person, otherwise scammers will enroll multiple times under different names to multiply their benefits. To guard against that, the agency needs to check all 10 fingers and both irises of each person against those on its records. If, as planned, 600 million peopled have been logged by 2014, that'll entail running about 14 billion matches per second. And, as always with IT, problems won't be clear until they actually show up. Programming flaws that delay each request unnoticeably when only a small number of queries is being run can become a real headache with heavy volume. Aardhaar has already found that when about 5,000 queries a day were being entered answers came back in a fraction of a second, but with 20,000 requests the delay increased dramatically. And all this against the backdrop of the chronically intermittent electricity supply and frequent collapse of servers that anyone using a computer in India is only too familiar with.

Then there is anarchic India's genius in bending every conceivable rule. Some iris-scanners can be fooled by a high-quality photo pasted onto a contact lens, while fingerprints can be lifted from almost anything you touch and a laser-printed reproduction will have tiny ridges of ink that may fool scanners. And there is always the scruffy envelope: an Aadhaar operative could simply be bribed to match a scan scammer's name with someone else's biometrics. But, no system is perfect if human beings have anything to do with it, and a useful analogy might be with credit cards. Card numbers are stolen all the time, but everyone still uses the service because the card companies have come up with fairly good ways to spot fraudulent use. Overall, fraud in the system is a relatively small price to pay for its huge benefits; presumably the same calculus will hold for Aadhaar.

Predictably, the whole idea of Aadhaar horrifies civil libertarians. Protesters recently picketed Nilekani's speech at the National Institute of Advanced Studies; several anti-Aadhaar websites have sprung up. MP's and prominent intellectuals have criticized the scheme, just as they did in the UK, Canada and Australia earlier this year when those countries had to put their plans for a biometric ID card on the back burner. Technically, Aadhaar is voluntary but in practice, once the system really takes hold, it will be extremely difficult for anyone to function without being part of it. Arundhati Roy, former novelist and current cover-girl for the intellectual left, finds it 'obnoxious and frightening', pointing that in India people have often been targeted for discrimination because of their religion or caste. Nilekani would disagree: "In our situation, our whole focus is on delivering benefits to people. It's all about making your life easier" he says. The Unique Identification Authority is very deliberately not collecting information on anyone's race or caste, but local governments and other agencies subcontracted to collect data are permitted to ask questions about race or caste and link the information they harvest to the respondent's Aadhaar number. And while the agency itself has pledged not to share data with security or other government agencies, how can this be guaranteed?

Being realistic, to expect no wider use of such a potent system is naïve, at best. Security is obviously a major concern in India today: witness the proliferation of armed guards, x-ray machines, and metal detectors at airports, shopping centers and even the capital's smart new underground stations. If you drive into the grounds of a fancy cosmopolitan hotel these days, not only are mirrors shone under the car's chassis but its boot and bonnet are opened up too. You cannot blame the Indian authorities. 2008 saw the Mumbai terror attacks; then Kashmiri separatists bombed and murdered at the national Parliament in Delhi. In 2010 alone there were three major jihadist incidents: a shooting at Old Delhi's Jama Masjid mosque, serial bombs outside Bangalore's Chinnaswami stadium and the bombing of the German cafe in Pune. Moreover India has chronically hostile neighbours on each flank: Pakistan and China. The latter, the Dalai Lama issue apart, may appear conciliatory, but the last few years have seen a surreptitious advance of its influence from occupied Tibet into Maoist-dominated Nepal. In India herself, the government has 35 terror groups banned and there are currently localized civil wars against assorted left-wing groups (all bearing Chinese weapons) in no less than sixty districts around the country: Chhattisgarh, West Bengal, Bihar, Jharkhand, Orissa, Assam, Andhra Pradesh — you name it. Manipur, a tiny north-eastern state unknown to the outside world, saw 246 terrorist related incidents in the first three months of 2012, seven times the level of disturbance in headline-grabbing Kashmir. And of course, terror cells are always bubbling among the 12% of the Indian population that is Muslim. Often poor and uneducated, their disaffected young make ideal jihadist warriors.

Candid police officials have told the press that they would love to use Aadhaar information in their fight against crime, arguing that this would only be an extension of existing surveillance. In Chattisgarh, for example, local police are implementing a scheme whereby any customers buying certain things — electrical goods and over 200 feet of wire for example — must have their fingerprints taken by the shopkeeper. These ink impressions will be kept to help identify apprehended Maoists in the area. Even Nilekani admits "We would share data for national security purposes, but there will be processes for that so you have checks and balances". He points out that as mobile phones can be tapped and tracked, it could be said that the country already has an infant surveillance state, and adds "When you have hundreds of millions of people who are not getting access to basic services, isn't that more important than some imagined risk?"

Civil liberties arguments must seem meaningless to Laxmi, who is looking forward to using her Aadhaar number to obtain a government card for the subsidized groceries available to those poor who can prove they live in Delhi. It will also exempt her from the frequent police purges aimed at clearing non-residents from the overcrowded slum where she lives. But of course, not everyone in India is poor. Just as her eyes have given Laxmi a new lease of life, her fashionista sisters in Mumbai are hoping to use theirs to improve their own fortunes. However, their preferred contact lenses do not have fake irises pasted on them but real diamonds — eighteen of them, fetchingly set into plates of white or yellow gold. Sales are booming; a distributor for the UK is being sought. And the cost of these trendy accessories? A mere £10,000. Or, in Laxmi's case, about thirty years hard work sorting cast-off clothes …

21

Jai Italistan!

IF YOU WANT to understand India in European terms, take a look at Italy. There are many similarities between the two countries. Both are ancient civilisations that have just about seen it all and have few illusions about humanity. Both are deeply steeped in religion, with the result that they demonstrate congenital piety and cynical pragmatism in just about equal measure. Both were for centuries a group of independent and often competing princely states and neither has been a single nation, with any clear idea of what that means, for very long. Italy only became united due to Garibaldi's efforts at the end of the nineteenth century and India had to wait more than another fifty years to become a single country. As a result, both continue to boast strong regional identities and differences, celebrated, for example, in thriving local traditions of cuisine. This proud regionalism is compounded in the subcontinent's case by her quite extraordinarily variegated make-up — linguistic, cultural and religious. The downside for the Centre at Delhi is that states are queuing up for more autonomy, or even, in some cases, secession from the Union. Italy, of course, has the ever-cantankerous Northern League with its plan to cut the despised south adrift.

In both countries the traditional importance of the family, often run by a strong woman, is still paramount. And partly because of this, in neither country will you find the Anglo-Saxon assumption that a person is primarily an independent individual whose duty is to carve his or her way through life. What counts is the group. To be is to be part of a group, and without such an affiliation it is virtually impossible to survive. The primary group is the family, an amorphous and hydra-headed creature and particularly so in India. The huge family crowd at any wedding will demonstrate this, as do the specific terms used in Indian languages to designate multiple near and distant relations: elder sister, younger brother, mother's cousin etc. Then, like so many concentric circles surrounding the individual, come many secondary 'families' that simultaneously succour and restrain him: caste, *gotra* (i.e. family groups of castes), trade union, political party. And speaking of politics, both countries are quite mad about them. Centuries under the yoke of religious and aristocratic domination have bequeathed both Indians and Italians that fascination with power only to be found in those habituated to seeing themselves as powerless.

The fact is, neither India nor Italy has fully developed the post-Hobbesian concept of the State as a centralised and generally benign institution that is worth supporting by paying taxes and from which one can expect basic amenities and reliable help. For these one turns to the family, and the tax levied is your independence. It is family not State that is the first port of call when you are ill, lose your job or need to pay for schooling. The State, along with its functionaries, has for centuries been deeply mistrusted as either distant and uninterested or arrogant and interfering. And the converse of this, in both countries, is that political office is not seen primarily as a means of helping one's fellow citizens through joining a trustworthy institution and exercising a power legitimated through the ballot box, but as a purchasable means of furthering one's own advantage and that of one's immediate and extended family.

In Italy the historic consequence of this distrust in a central State was that people looked elsewhere for some semblance of governance and support, and into the gap stepped various groups of regional fixers: the Mafia, Camorra and 'Ndrangheta. Such organisations first insinuated themselves into their compatriots' hearts and minds by getting things done locally when absent or lazy politicians couldn't or wouldn't; only later did they turn into the vast criminal networks which, even today, still handle much day-to-day government on the ground. This is why the Mafia is known as Cosa Nostra, i.e. it is *our* thing, as opposed to their thing, 'they' being the distant bureaucrats in Rome or the far north.

Indians too are fed up with the arterial sclerosis in the body politic, the endless paperwork and anonymous envelopes (or their equivalents) that have to pass from hand to hand before one can receive various civic entitlements and obtain legitimate 'permissions' in life and business. There are limits even to India's patience; witness the huge appeal of Anna Hazare's clean up corruption bandwagon. In the subcontinent though, the mafia (to use the term generically) has not just remained behind the political scenes as backer and string-puller but moved directly into the electoral process. A couple of examples: at the last general election, exercising a curiously generous civil freedom allowed by the Indian constitution, no less than eight parliamentary candidates stood for re-election from behind prison bars, three of them on murder charges.

And in the March 2012 polls conducted for five State Assemblies — Uttar Pradesh, Manipur, Punjab, Uttarakhand and Goa — 35% of those elected had criminal backgrounds. Only Manipur elected members who had no cases pending against them while Uttar Pradesh topped the list with 47% of her new Assembly members under charges of breaking the law. The *victor ludorum* in this charade is surely one Mitra Sen of UP's Samajwadi party, a low-caste conglomerate led by ageing former wrestler Mulayam Singh Yadav. Sen had thirty-six cases pending against him. These dismal figures are no doubt partly explained by the widespread launching of a lawsuit as a political weapon, but nonetheless smoke, fire and all that...

Those interested in the political tentacles emanating from India's lurid underworld will enjoy *Shantaram* by Gregory David Roberts. How much is true and how much made up, I have no idea, but it's a cracking read and at just under a thousand pages of smallish print, there's enough there to keep you going for several long journeys, including both Indian and Italian-style delays.

It must be said in defence of the subcontinent that at least she does not share Italy's disastrous taste in leaders. Political chiefs here tend to be elderly by Western standards, and perhaps because of her long tradition of respecting age and wisdom — what we might call the '*guru* syndrome' — independent India has chosen a succession of rather admirable and statesman-like leaders. Pandit Nehru, Indira Gandhi, (possibly her son Rajiv had he lived long enough), Narasingha Rao and, particularly, Atal Bihari Vajpayee are some who come to mind. By contrast, the Italian electorate resembles some serially battered wife who repeatedly chooses an abuser, because for some dark and hidden reason, that is what she really wants. The result? First there was Mussolini, then Andreotti, Craxi, Berlusconi — what a motley ragbag of assorted clowns, gangsters and spivs!

Leaving aside Italy, an intriguing question: does the 'family first' mind-set make political corruption endemic to south Asians? Well, a south Asian, in fact no less a figure than UK Conservative party chairman, the Baroness Lady Warsi, certainly thinks so. In an interview in the New Statesman magazine in 2010 the refreshingly direct peer made explosive accusations about electoral fraud, claiming it was particularly rife amongst the Asian community. This was quite a shock; any white Brit saying the same would have been pilloried for racism. Nevertheless, the facts remain: a far higher proportion of south Asians than their total numbers in office would suggest have recently got into trouble with corruption in UK politics. Three Asian-UK members of the House of Lords, Amirali Bhatia, Pola Uddin and Swaraj Paul, were all found to have breached expenses rules by claiming on houses that were not their main homes, and another report the same year busted eight Brit-Asian MPs for fiddling their expenses.

Then in the spring of 2012 it transpired that, in some spookily apt confirmation of her own accusations and as a result of the fallout from a personal row with a south Asian donor and fundraiser, Lady Warsi was herself rumbled. She was accused both of receiving expenses for renting a flat near her work which she pocketed while actually staying rent-free with a friend, and also for failing to follow the law by telling the House of Lords authorities that she was receiving income from a London property she had bought and rented out. This rent was on top of her handsome salary paid by the Conservative party and the £300 a day allowance she legitimately claimed when she actually attended their lordships' noble chamber. As these were exactly the sort of breaches of parliamentary guidelines that have damaged many British MP's of all stripes over the last two or three years, the whole event was a headline embarrassment. It was further compounded when it emerged that Lady Varsi had taken a relative with her on a government trip to Pakistan, as this man owned a business (in which she also had shares) that stood to profit from such high level introductions. The complex situation was not defused by Lady Varsi's trotting out the phrase we have become all too accustomed to hearing in such situations: "I take full responsibility for my unfortunate oversight". This is a meaningless tautology; if a sane adult does not take full responsibility for their actions, who on earth is meant to?

Enough of this — *basta* as the Italians would say, or *bas* as the Indians do. I shall close the delicate subject forthwith, before some politically correct mafiosi come knocking on my door in the dead of night to make me an offer I can't refuse …

22

Life is all give and take

HOT ON THE heels of the FIFA bribery fiasco, we hear news of a novel idea to address the curious and all-too universal confusion between public duty and private gain. Moreover, it comes from a country not totally unfamiliar with the problem: India. To give them their due Indians, unlike the British, do not adopt genteel euphemisms such as 'sleaze' to kid themselves that real 'corruption' is something that happens elsewhere, but manfully admit to the problem, albeit with a rueful smile and resigned shrug. Now comes a bold solution, and from a government expert no less. In a recent paper posted on the Finance Ministry's official website, one Kaushil Basu advises that to reduce bribery, the act of bribing should be made legal. Just to repeat: legal.

Innovative thinker Basu argues that if bribe-giving is legalised, while bribe-taking remains illegal, bribe-givers will have an incentive to blow the whistle after paying up. Knowing this, bribe-takers will hesitate to take bribes. Hmm…A moment's thought reveals this proposal to be morally suspect. Not only does it condone bribe-giving, it also relies on bribers being doubly corrupt: first by bribing and secondly by stabbing bribe-takers in the back.

In fact the more one studies Basu's assumption that legalising bribery will cause it to decline the more it appears, frankly, to be bonkers. How so? Well, let's take it step by step. A bribe-giver would actually have not two options — i.e. 'bribe' or 'don't bribe' — but three: (1) don't pay a bribe; (2) bribe and whistle-blow and (3) bribe but don't whistle-blow. Basu claims his proposal enhances the attractiveness of option 2 as against option 1. However, it actually makes option 3 the most attractive of the lot: the briber is not penalised if caught and his conscience is also clear since bribing is not illegal. It is easy to construct examples where the effect of the proposal would be a switch from the first to the third option, leading to an actual increase in bribery!

Let us consider someone who is tempted to pay a bribe to get a telephone line installed, often a lengthy and tedious business here. Suppose that the consequences of blowing the whistle are protracted litigation with huge costs, possible harassment and little chance of getting justice — sadly not a far-fetched assumption. In this situation, paying a bribe and blowing the whistle is not much of an option, even if bribe-giving is legal. The real choice is between not paying a bribe, and paying a bribe without blowing the whistle. It is perfectly possible that many people would choose the former if bribing were illegal and punishable, but the latter if bribe-giving were legalised.

Indeed, the more Basu's case is examined, the less logic it has. His paper ends with a plea to his fellow countrymen (whose homeland ranked 78th on Transparency International's latest index): "if we want to really get at corruption, what we need to build up are values of honesty and integrity in society". Fair enough. But how can the legalisation of bribe-giving make it less immoral? If it did, surely that would tend to encourage, not discourage, bribing. And if not, why would anyone blow the whistle after paying a bribe? That would be in effect drawing attention to one's own immorality. Basu even suggests that agent provocateur bribers might be "reimbursed" if they blow the whistle, a suggestion that takes us ever further into cloud cuckoo land.

Barmy left-field though it may be, Kaushik Basu's paper is symptomatic of a disease all too common in the economics profession: the tendency to make sweeping policy recommendations based on analytical models that have a very limited domain of validity. What you end up with is confusion worse confounded. So as life is all give and take, perhaps it would be easier just to continue business as usual? Then pass me that grubby envelope, would you ...

23

Long live Indinglish, isn't it?

SEVERAL YEARS AGO some earnest twit working for the British Council in Delhi had a grand scheme. He resolved to abolish Indian–English — that fantabulous hybrid found all over the subcontinent — in newspapers, official notices, advertisements, menus — and get all Indians to speak The Queen's English 'properly'. The reason for such an ambitious project was depressingly utilitarian: 'to enable Indians to engage more successfully in international business'. In entertaining such a hubristic fantasy, the hapless bureaucrat displayed ignorance quite unworthy of his employer, which is by and large a pretty worthy institution. Not unsurprisingly, the scheme was a total flop.

There were several key facts the man from the Council had overlooked. To begin with it should not be forgotten that India has vast numbers who already speak English excellently. Everyday experience in the country will show this, and it is not surprising, for the Indians are natural linguists. Let alone English, many of them are fluent in two or three or more Indian languages as different from each other as are those of Europe, and thereby display a facility compared to which Britain's tongue-tied insularity is a downright embarrassment. Moreover, even a glance at contemporary Indian literature will reveal that some of the best English being written today is being written by Indians. Among the magical realists, of whom Salman Rushdie is the most celebrated, one finds ample evidence of an almost Victorian ear for the weight of a word, the rhythm of a line, while at the other end of the spectrum, the pellucid simplicity of expression in R. K. Narayan's novels is an absolute delight. His *Malgudi* books chronicling the ups and downs of everyday life in the eponymous and fictional small south Indian town, should be required reading for anyone hoping to master the scribe's craft. Again, this facility is not to be wondered at. Indians are, after all, the inheritors of the world's greatest tradition of storytelling and one which is still, just, alive. And above and beyond this is the larger picture that our myopic Council man missed: a language, God help us all, does not just exist for 'doing business' — well, not quite yet anyway.

Just as huge numbers of Indians speak immaculate English so the number that uses various hybrid forms of it is also rather large and, this being India, is probably increasing shamelessly. Any attempt to regulate this remorseless organic growth was bound to fail. Looking back in time, it did not take long for Indian languages and English to combine and form a means of communication that was used by those members of the Raj who came into close working contact with native Indians. By 1882 this Anglo-Indian tongue was enough of a language in its own right to merit its own lexicon, the classic *Hobson Jobson — A Glossary of Colloquial Anglo-Indian Words and Phrases* which is still in print. (If you want a taste of it, try Amitav Ghosh's Booker shortlisted novel *Sea of Poppies*). Today the colonial hybrid of Anglo –Indian has changed again, and the newer greatly streamlined version has become, in practice, just one member of the subcontinent's vibrant family of over eight hundred minor tongues. Providing a means of communication for millions, it has its own history, its own conventions, its own eccentric and considerable charm. Let us call it Indinglish.

In the days when I used to teach my native tongue to non-native speakers, it was known as English as a Foreign Language (EFL) and the idea was to impart set grammatical rules and a more or less received pronunciation. Nowadays the EFL model no longer holds absolute sway and in the world of language teaching what matters it is what people actually say, not what they may be trying, and in many cases failing, to say. Distinctions such as that between singular and plural with their corresponding verb endings seem to be no longer considered important and grammatical mistakes are not considered wrong, just different, creative even. According to this view what was once called Pidgin English should officially be known as English as a Second Language (ESL) and I'm sure there will soon be undergraduate courses in it. Fine, *pace* the purists, language is always changing, so let the modern descendant of Anglo-Indian, Indinglish, assume its rightful place in the newly honoured ranks of ESL.

As the British Raj established itself across the subcontinent, English gradually replaced Persian as the language of the ruler, just as Persian had replaced Sanskrit three hundred years earlier when Islam arrived in force. Language played an increasingly important role in the Raj's ambition to unify the plurality of its new dominion under the banner of Western Christian Civilisation. The advance of this attempted linguistic takeover can be traced to the famous government Minute of 1835 in which the most energetic promoter of English as the imperial *lingua franca*, the historian Thomas Babington Macaulay, advances the idea in disingenuously altruistic terms:

'The problem in India is that we have to educate a people who cannot at present be educated by means of their mother tongue. We must teach them some foreign language'

After lauding the English language and the civilisation that lies behind it, Macaulay concludes:

'Whether we look at the intrinsic value of our literature or at the particular situation of India, we shall see the strongest reason to think that of all foreign tongues, the English tongue is that which would be the most useful to our native subjects'.

And not just to them, one might add.

Fifty years later a letter to London from the then Viceroy, Frederick Hamilton-Temple-Blackwood 1st Marquess of Dufferin and Ava, advocates the infusion of English into the very fabric of governance and thence everyday life:

'There is no reason why English terms should not be adopted to describe the subdivision of jurisdiction, the Courts of justices, the rank of officials and the operations of Commerce, Manufacture and Agriculture...'.

This triple-barrelled salvo did the trick, but an unintended consequence was that Raj English was soon to spawn a half-caste surrogate: Indinglish. Using the language of the foreign elite, however approximately, gave the native writer a certain authority and status, it aligned him with the dominant power in the land, particularly in the large urban centres to which the Raj's power remained largely confined. In commercial enterprises, Indinglish immediately placed the goods on offer at the high end of the market and advertisers were quick to see the advantage of such a sophisticated pitch. This was especially so amongst those peddling folk and quack medicines, who perhaps needed their powers of persuasion boosted more than most. Thus in 1895 The Madras Standard, for example, carried a delicately worded advertisement for an aphrodisiac, a 'power pill' with the impressively Latinate name of *Pilula Poentia*:

'a sovereign remedy for nervous debility, premature decay of Vitality loss of manhood. It also purifies the blood, revives the drooping and languishing spirit of the despondent, impart tone and vigour to the weak frame...'

Over a hundred and twenty years later, a local Bombay newspaper in early 2012 would address the same age-old problem, but with a frankness of language and a pitch mixing tradition and technology that is brazenly contemporary:

'Sex Problem: Why Disappointed? Japani men Organ Developer Free For men Organ Developer Inlargement Effect on your Organ Developer within 6 Hours Get rid of problems like small, slim, non straight organ developer. Make internal organ 7–8 inch long, thick & hard. Increase Sex Time Upto 40 to 55 Minutes. Masti Oil, Excitement Capsule, Romantic Spry, 175 Kama Kala Book/DVD/8GBMemory Card. Female Tomer Cream Free with 45 days medicine.'

The ad goes on to assure readers that the product is:

'100% Ayurvedic & guarantee benefit. No Side Effect. Money back Guaranteed Offer.'

The intervening years may have removed much of the subtlety and reserve, but the language used is still, we might say, admirably virile.

Indinglish suited the claims of those peddling spiritual cures too. A wonderfully evocative visual record of the country around the time of her Independence is provided by *Henri Cartier-Bresson in India*. One of the master's immaculately composed black and white canvases from 1947 shows an astrologer in his shop in the millworking area of Bombay. While his shelves display rows of skulls, his notice-board advertises:

'Great Care of all Sarts of Diseases without medicine or troubles or pains which may be ailing you. If you are over come-d by jadu* or Bhoot**, palit. If you are out of Emp-loyment or Business go Slack & Not sho-wing any profit. Children do not live your heart, besides…'

This last truncated phrase, like so much Indinglish, has a ring of gravitas, wisdom even, but leaves its meaning to dangle tantalisingly in thin air.

Not only roadside *fakirs*, but some companies that later became household names happily used Indinglish to promote their wares. At about the same time Cartier Bresson was 'clicking', as Indinglish has it, the future international giant Parke Davis was also on the revitalizing bandwagon, promising the readers of its advertisements that the herbal tonic called Octagon would deliver:

'surprising increase in vitality and energy within the first 24 hours. It makes

*black magic   **an evil spirit

a man or woman look and feel 15 to 20 years younger than the actual age...'

Such vertiginously ambitious claims were perhaps occasioned by the enervation that India's climate caused Westerners, but were doubtless bolstered by the fact that they were being made in a medium that had the allure of both novelty and authority.

English has the most words of any language — the Oxford English dictionary lists almost half a million — but some can behave in downright illogical ways. Why, for example, don't 'enough', 'plough', 'cough', 'through' 'ought' and 'although' all rhyme? No two do. And then there are phrasal verbs, which, as I'm sure you will remember from your schooldays, are those pesky verbs followed by a preposition that are always turning up *(sic)* in English. Indinglish loves to shuffle the prepositions around inventively: monsoon rain regularly turns cricket matches into a 'wash up', old belongings get 'tossed off', unsuccessful tv quiz contestants get 'knocked up', useless employees get 'kicked off' from their jobs. Aspiring Bollywood starlettes are known as 'struggle-ups'. It's a delightful neologism; presumably when times get hard and these ambitious young ladies moonlight as 'models' they morph silkily into 'snuggle-ups'.

Indinglish often has its own instinctual logic, albeit initially obscure, that confirms what the ever-astute James Cameron in his classic memoir *Indian Summer*, referred to as "the Indian gift of knowing what words mean." Take our word 'pair', which should mean two of something but often refers to just one object that happens to have two identical parts. Indinglish will have none of this confusion, brusquely rendering a pair of trousers as 'one pant'. Similarly, I remember asking a hotel receptionist if I could borrow a pair of scissors. She bent under the desk to look, then popped up again with a quizzical expression: 'Would that be one scissor you want, or two?'

Sometimes the logic takes some figuring out. If you ask directions in India, you may well be given the answer in 'furlongs' — an Anglo Saxon term derived from ploughing not used for many decades in Britain, though I do remember learning it by rote in tables at school, there were eight to a mile as I recall. But, being more or less a composite of the words 'far' and 'long', I guess the term well conveys a general sense of indeterminate distance, which is just how Indinglish uses it.

Walking too many furlongs may put you in a mood for some sleep, but don't expect an establishment calling itself an 'hotel' to offer accommodation, places so advertised usually offer only food. But if it is only food you want, you may sometimes see a sign announcing a 'Rest au Rent'. At first glance this appears to be just an Indinglish misspelling of Restaurant, which would be fair enough — it is after all the most frequently mis-spelt word in internet search engines. But on closer consideration, we realize that a restaurant, as well as providing food, also offers a couple of hours when one can relax and take the weight off one's feet. Ergo, you are renting a rest. QED.

This refreshing establishment may well have an 'A/C Dinning Room'. The A/C (air-conditioning) will surely turn it into a fridge, but, contrary to expectations, it may not be noisy and may even enjoy a 'pindrop silence'. The menu can offer 'Tomato Soap' (a very good starter for those concerned with hygiene) followed by a choice from intriguing sections such as 'Quadrupeps', 'The Winged Flock' or 'Vegeatables'. Not very hungry? Then the 'Snakes' section may proffer 'Assort Sand Witches' or a 'Chilly Cheese Toast' (which sounds cold but turns out to be fiery). Best of all you may have the chance of a 'Home Late'. When the latter dish arrives it turns out to be three eggs beaten together and fried. Of course! When one gets home late, too late for a full dinner, whisking up a quick omelette is just the answer. And after your meal, the establishment's probably rather bedraggled garden may well display a notice that forbids 'plucking of flowers'; however, such sternness is not infrequently offset by another sign encouraging the visitor to 'enjoy fun and frolic'.

Coquette or not, Indinglish can certainly be a shameless flatterer. Someone may be complimented as looking 'princelified', especially if they are dressed up and on their way to some 'jollification', while the overweight may considerately be described as 'plumpy' or, even more tactfully 'plumpish'. It can also console. At breakfast I was once told that toast wasn't available as the electric toaster was broken. As a longtime devotee of a good breakfast I must have looked disappointed, for the waiter returned a few minutes later bearing an air of triumph and a plate of white bread: 'Sir, plain toast is available!'.

Indinglish lends authority to official notices, to which it adds a veneer of transparency and even incorruptibility, qualities to be welcomed in anything to do with government here. But veneer it is; the fact is that many of the people to whom these notices are ostensibly addressed will not actually be able to read them. Still, their self-assurance remains for they have done their duty in stating a laudable intention. Take a notice published in the Hindustan Times of 2005 by the government of Uttaranchal on the subject of driving safely on that state's mountainous roads. Part of it reads:

'Driver should no consume any intoxication like alcohol etc. Drivers will be checked on breath analysers of interceptors and if found intoxicated Steam action will be taken against such driver and vehicle owner'.

As so often in Indinglish, a majestic capital letter emphasises clearly the important word, but what the phrase actually means remains a mystery.

Educating the citizens of Delhi in the use of escalators has produced the following classically unpunctuated notice displayed in the capital's main railway station, though its breathlessness makes riding an escalator sound far more exhausting than climbing any amount of stairs:

GUIDANCE FOR SAFE TRAVEL ON ESCALaTORS

'While climbing escalators put right leg on moving stairs and hold handrail and put other leg immediately on moving stairs while climbing down put right leg on stationary plate and leave the handrail and put other leg on stationary plate'

And what about that lapse into lower case 'a' in the upper-cased title? Could it be an artful depiction of descending (from the previous capital letter) and ascending (to the next), a clever visual reinforcement of meaning inserted to relieve the compositor's boredom and/or grab the reader's attention? I like to think so. At the least, it well illustrates India's love of the curlicue, a preference everywhere observable in both her art and her life.

The best popular account of Indinglish I know is the intriguingly titled *'Entry from Backside Only'*. This not uncommon sign, as author Binoo K. John points out, refers to accessing a building rather than anything more salacious. Mr. John, a Keralite working in Delhi, is in a good position to know about all this as he is a well-respected journalist and daily newspapers have been enormously influential in legitimizing the use of Indinglish ever since its inception, and they still are. Open any paper here and you will find that 'cops have nabbed miscreants' who were perhaps 'eve-teasers'*, 'undertrials'** or 'history-sheeters't. Whether they were attempting to 'abscond' and 'flee into a godown'‡ or just 'quacking in their boots with fear' such 'riff-raff' were no match for 'the uniformed sleuths'. Or you might learn that a particular district is witnessing an alarming increase in 'hookers'. This has nothing to do with a rise in sexual peccadilloes but refers to the fact that more and more free-loaders are avoiding bills by attaching their own leads to power or phone lines registered in other peoples' names.

* sexual harassers   ** those on bail
† those with a criminal record   ‡ warehouse

Readers' letters have long employed some spectacular Indinglish. The classic example is one I came across thirty years ago and it remains unequalled. Mr. Okhil Chandra Sen writes to the Bengal Railways Company in 1909:

> 'Sir, I am arrive by passenger train Ahmedpur station and my belly is too much swelling with jackfruit. I am therefore went to privy. Just as I doing the nuisance that guard making whistle blow for train to go off and I am running with lotah (i.e. water pot) in one hand and dhoti in the next when I am fall over and expose all my shocking to man and female women on platform. This too much bad, if passenger go to make dung that dam guard not wait train five minutes for him. I am therefore pray your honour to make big fine on that guard for public sake. Otherwise I am making big report to the papers'.

History does not relate whether 'that dam guard' was fined, but Mr. Sen's 'big report' has assured him a well-earned place in posterity.

In our times of globalization, mass-immigration and intermarriage, the idea of having one fixed identity is fracturing. Language must increasingly reflect this, so it is no surprise to see Indinglish has now reincarnated in a new form amongst the South Asian diaspora in the UK. This latest overlap of the English and Indian languages there has become known as Hinglish and, like the Spanglish found throughout the Latino-Mexican immigrated parts of the United States, it is thriving. The most pervasive and best-known of Hinglish words is 'innit?'. The origin of this little fellow is rather complex, but bear with me as I don my chalk-dusted EFL mortar-board and attempt to explain its genesis.

Most languages have what are called 'question tags' that are stuck on the end of sentences as a reinforcing agent. In some they are invariable, such as the French *n'est-ce pas* ? or the German *nicht wahr* ?, but English, always a tricky creature, has many different 'question tags', which are formed by repeating a preceding verb in its negative form. Thus, if the first verb is a form of 'to be', it is simply repeated, as in: "It's hot, isn't it?", "We are late, aren't we?", "She will be there, won't she?". But if the first verb is not a form of 'to be', the repeated verb is generally a negative form of 'to do', as in: "You like toast, don't you?", "We took the wrong turn, didn't we?" "She lives in London, doesn't she?" and so on. (It gets more complicated, but let's leave it there, shall we?). Now Hindi, like French and German, has only one tag: *hai na* which means "isn't it?", an invariant used in all cases, and often abbreviated to *na*. This tag, transferred to Indinglish, gives us: 'You are tired, isn't it?' or 'She likes curry, isn't it?' etc. Added to this we must take into account Indinglish's ineradicable preference for the present continuous over the present simple, a tricky distinction many languages don't have. Thanks to this preference, the English 'You like music, don't you?' is finally transformed into the Indinglish 'You are liking music, isn't it?' Presto!

Hinglish, meanwhile, being a younger, hipper and lazier relative of Indinglish, takes things a step further by eliding the invariant 'isn't it?' into the nonchalantly cool 'innit?'. This semantic cockroach scuttles, indestructible, into all sorts of situations to imply all sorts of things: assent, irony, approval, emphasis. On its own as a duosyllabic grunt it implies general street solidarity.

Pre-eminently a language of the young, Hinglish is always evolving new forms to fit the new means of communication. If a Hinglish speaker has to get somewhere in a hurry, he might make an 'airdash'; if she needs to bring a meeting forward, she does the opposite of postponing and 'prepones'. If you are reading this when you should be at your desk working, you are indulging in a 'timepass'. Just as Indinglish in its time was kept alive in the subcontinent through advertising, official notices, the media and Bollywood, so Hinglish is being given a modern spin and international reach through music channels, the internet and satellite TV hits such as 'Goodness Gracious Me' and 'The Kumars at Number 42'.

Researchers have found that many second generation British Indians now switch between using 'prestige English' (i.e. correct English delivered in the dulcet tones of received pronunciation) and Hinglish, depending on the situation. The former is used in formal situations, such as work or during an interview, the latter when at home surrounded by friends and family. This phenomenon of inhabiting two quite separate linguistic worlds with two different identities is, interestingly, found predominantly among young women.

Recently, many NRI's (which stands for Non-Resident Indians, though to some it denotes Not Really Indian) have begun returning to the subcontinent in numbers to look after ageing relatives. And with them, Hinglish is coming back home to reinvigorate its own ageing parent. Not long ago, no less a cultural commentator than the Times of India celebrated this re-spicing of what the writer Suleiman Rushdie has well called the 'chutneyfication' of the English language when it reported: 'Brand India has shaken, stirred and otherwise Bangalored the world's consciousness.' Yes, 'to Bangalore' is Hinglish for to send overseas or outsource, as in call-centres. It seems everything is going round in circles.

Speaking of which, throughout the summer of 2006 the following advertisement ran in the prestigious Economic Times for CD Roms teaching the latest skills of business communication to the young hopefuls of the New India:

'We will continue to sapply profit to darling customers, holders of shares, staff gentleman (also ladis) and the vendor type people.'

So, I think we can all safely assume that by now the hapless Canute of the British Council must be feeling like a drowned rat, isn't it?

24

Long obsolete olisboi

A RECENT MAGAZINE article on the female orgasm claimed that 60% of women under the age of fifty in the UK now own a vibrator. The author, a woman, lauded the statistic as indicative of a new and welcomed 'independence and empowerment' among her sisters. As a man, and an increasingly grumpy old one to boot, I see it differently. To my mind such a statistic is merely another indication of our increasing emotional solipsism and our tendency to prefer spending time with machines rather than with living human beings. Of course, living human beings are harder to switch off, which I suppose is one reason they are losing out to gizmos.

Be that as it may, as a subscriber to the view that there is nothing new under the sun, I was set to thinking about the ancient Indian attitude to such matters. The ancient Indians were of course meticulous, if not obsessive, experimenters, investigators and recorders of pretty well everything imaginable, and sex was very much no exception. On the whole, Indian chroniclers gave sex-aids the thumbs down, as the general word for them in the *kama shastras*, the texts devoted to sensual pleasure, is *apadravya* which means 'a bad instrument'. Nevertheless, in practice, such implements seem to have been very popular, especially among both sodomites and sapphists, women in harems and solitary females such as widows, who according to Hindu custom generally could not remarry. For all such, a category called *kritima linga* 'artificial phalluses' was recommended, that included a variety of suitably botuliform eatables — radishes, aubergines, bananas and the like. Dildos of candle wax, baked clay, wood, bone or metal were also common. Krishna, the god of love, is said to have had 16,000 lovers. Perhaps not unsurprisingly, many of them were driven to ease their unfulfilled longings by skilfully employing figurines of their concupiscent lord. In the more mundane course of events, writers on erotics also recommend men to use such devices to stimulate their partner before intercourse, if so desired.

On the male side, there is a category of sex toy called *viyoni* 'without vagina', which were images of women made of wood and cloth with an appropriately shaped opening constructed of fruits, vegetables and leaves. Interestingly, such 'dolls' seem to have been chiefly used for fertility rites, as punishments are prescribed for men who resort to such artifices merely to gain pleasure.

The texts pay considerable attention to the remedying of impotence. If ayurvedic herbal remedies failed, one recommended device was an - appropriately shaped cast made of a number of materials — gold, silver, copper, iron, zinc, lead, wood or ivory. This had a roughened exterior and its tip was pierced with holes, rather like a salt cellar. Fitted over the penis it made up for any loss of strength, thus ensuring the recipient's satisfaction. Such implements were expensive; those who could not afford them are recommended to use a more basic device: a bamboo stalk of acceptable width, coated with oil and tied around the waist with a cord.

Those ancients with flagging powers seem to have taken great pains to satisfy their women. They employed gruesome procedures involving various types of implant that threatened to turn a man's marriage into a life-sentence of penile servitude. The second century author Vatsayana, in the chapter that deals with sex in his curiously mechanical manual on sense-pleasure, the *Kama Sutra*, makes the extraordinary claim that in his time penile implants were 'as common as piercing the ears of children'. He adds that this was especially so in south India. Leaving aside the fact that north Indians have always said strange things about their southern neighbours, it is undeniable that many kinds of implant are described in detail in writings on the sexual life. All of them employ the insertion into the member of progressively larger pieces of twig over a long time until a permanent aperture is created, large enough to accommodate pieces of metal or wood of various sizes and shapes that can be inserted according to what the woman desires. Such devices are also found in Burma, Malaysia and Bali and other places where Indian . culture penetrated.

Perhaps the technique that gave most jollification was the implanting of tiny bells into the penis. Made of gold, silver or bronze — a familiar metallurgical hierarchy denoting the status of the owner — they were sewn onto a young boy, and periodically changed for larger ones as he grew. European travellers in India up to the sixteenth century witnessed this custom, and add that the selling and attaching of such bells was the job of a special caste of senior women, who often fitted a dozen or more to their customer. The bells tinkled charmingly as their owner strode jauntily along, and men so endowed were considered extremely attractive by the ladies. History does not relate whether these musical metallic appendages gave their recipients an added frisson of 'independence and empowerment' but at least those who used them didn't have to worry about the batteries going flat…

25

Man weds dog

IT WAS Groucho Marx who once complained that he had been married by a judge but should have asked for a jury. However, a man in our neighbouring state Tamil Nadu had no such regrets recently when he tied the knot, even though his bride was a real bitch.

In a bid to atone for killing two dogs in his younger days, 33-year-old P Selvakumar married stray pooch Selvi. The happy groom told a reporter from The Hindustan Times that he believed he had been cursed after stoning two dogs to death and hanging their bodies from a tree 15 years ago. Since committing that cruel act, he has suffered from paralysis in his legs and hands and lost the hearing in one ear. He explained that a local astrologer had informed him that marrying a dog was the only way to atone for his action and cure his maladies. Selvakumar's situation is not as uncommon as it may sound; people in rural India do sometimes organize a wedding to dogs and other animals, believing it can ward off certain curses.

Members of Selvakumar's family selected a four-year-old mongrel bitch, named her Selvi, and bathed and clothed her in preparation for the ceremony. According to reports, the bride looked resplendent in her orange wedding sari and flower garland. The reception, attended by some 200 guests, was held for the newly-weds in the groom's house. However, during the proceedings the idea of lifelong commitment seems to have given the bride cold feet — all four of them, presumably — as Selvi grew increasingly restless and then absconded. She was eventually nabbed and returned to her would-be husband, who forgave her wedding-day nerves and welcomed her back with a present of milk and a large bun, which she evidently enjoyed. The groom and his family then enjoyed their own celebratory feast.

Such a wedding is particularly interesting in that dogs are usually considered ritually unclean in India, and not treated particularly well. This may be partly due to the fact that in ancient lore, the only god associated with dogs was Yama, Lord of Death and the underworld. He has several watchdogs; possibly they are the Indian version of the West's 'hounds of hell'. Even today in some parts of the country bodies of the deceased are shown to dogs before being cremated or buried. Only one classical deity has a dog as his companion, and that is Kala Bhairava ('The Terrible') a wild and fierce form of Shiva who, as Lord of Time, orchestrates destruction and hangs around the cremation grounds with his retinue of gruesome spirits.

It is said that there are places in Mumbai where the pooch is worshipped as Shiva's vehicle, but I know of only two temples with strong canine connections. One is a Bhairava shrine in Shiva's hometown of Varanasi. This place commemorates a protective guardian of the city known as the *kotwal* who is believed to do the rounds each night on an invisible dog, hounding evil-doers. It has an image of both the magistrate and his mount, and shops outside the temple sell little dogs made of sugar that are given in offering. The other dog-friendly shrine is the Parassini Kadavu temple near Kannur in central Kerala, a couple of hours south of Neeleshwar Hermitage. Here the deity is a localized, low-caste form of Shiva in the form of a tribal hunter known to Malayalis as Shri Muthappan. He is always accompanied by his dog, accepts fish and alcohol as offerings, and blesses his devotees each morning and evening by taking possession of the trance-mediums who serve as his officiating priests. The ritual is a somber occasion, watched in pin-drop silence by quite large numbers. Dogs are very much welcome to attend and they usually appear right on time, tails wagging expectantly, when the bells ring to announce the ceremony.

The general Indian dislike of dogs tended to soften wherever there was extensive contact with Europeans and their pet-owning habits. Thus in the foothills, where the Raj decamped for the hot season and there were many army bases, dog-owning became quite common among Indians and still is. Recently the newly wealthy have also started adopting dogs as pets; at one time a particular favourite in Delhi was the pug, following a hugely successful Vodaphone advertising campaign that featured one. And now India is even beginning to breed the creatures; Dobermans, Alsatians, Labradors and Great Danes appear to be the most successful so far.

No doubt this would have pleased the dissolute Nawab of Junagadh, whose erstwhile state is now part of Gujarat. He did not marry a dog himself, but he did have one married. Among the many he owned, his favourite was a bitch called Rosana and when the time came for her to be mated, like any devoted father he decided she should be properly spliced but in the style of a royal princess. The marriage was conducted by *brahmin* priests and according to ancient Vedic rites. For her special day, the radiant bride was adorned with necklaces of pearls, rubies and gold, while her husband, one Bobby, was festooned in a cloth of the finest Mysore silk and his neck and ankles were hung with chains of solid gold. The ceremony was witnessed by 700 guests invited from all over India; the Viceroy was one of the few to decline the invitation, sniffily declaring the whole affair 'a piece of unprecedented silliness'. Silliness or no, a great time was had by all, and the celebrations were splendid. To commemorate the wedding, the Junagadh royal kennels were extended to 1000 dogs, and Roshana spent the rest of her days on velvet cushions in an air-conditioned apartment, fed on the choicest tit-bits served up on golden platters.

In the communal madness that followed Partition in 1947, Junagadh precipitously decided that his place as a Muslim was the newly-formed state of Pakistan. He fled Junagadh, leaving his wives and his people behind. He didn't desert his favourite dogs, however, and took a planeload with him. But perhaps Roshana never really felt happy on the other side of the border. Living off memories of her sumptuous wedding, perhaps she pined so much for her homeland that she ended up being reincarnated as Selvi?

26

Myth or reality?

THE TWO GREAT Oriental civilizations — India and China — have traditionally had very different attitudes to history. The Chinese have always been assiduous record keepers, believing 'The faintest ink is better than the clearest memory' and over the ages were fastidious in detailing the minutiae of family, dynasty and the celestial civil service that is the pantheon of their gods. The Indians on the other hand never took such great pains to preserve factual historical records, preferring to see history as a timeless and exemplary body of orally transmitted moral instruction rather than a painstaking log of the inevitable ups and downs of evanescent human life and society. When India has felt the need to consult a national historical record, she has tended to look to her two great epics, the Ramayana and Mahabharata, but as these voluminous works are crammed full of the escapades of assorted supernatural beings who shamelessly play very fast and loose with the rules of time, space and the mundane limits of common-sense, scholars, both Western and Westernised, have persistently dismissed them as mere 'mythology'.

However, science is now shedding some intriguing new light on the subject. Many events in the Mahabharata take place at Dwarka, the splendid capital of Lord Krishna, eighth incarnation of the great god Vishnu the preserver of the universe. This city, located on the coast of Gujarat, is popularly believed to have vanished at the height of its glory approximately five thousand years ago. Such a date is a millenium before any known Indian history, and is generally accepted as shorthand for a very long time ago. So, all romantic myth, said the experts. But then in 2001 marine excavations made by scientists conducting pollution studies in the Gulf of Cambay not far from the modern sacred city of Dwarka on the tip of the Gujarat peninsula, made an astonishing discovery. The remains of two man-made citadels the size of Manhattan, one eight and the other nine kilometers in length, were found sitting on the ocean bed. These ruins included stepped walls, platforms up to 100 metres in length, sophisticated right-angled structures and, as sub-seabed scanning showed, they rest on massive foundations under the existing ocean floor. As well as human jawbones and vertebrae many objects have been found:

tools, models of animals, pottery and ornaments. Carbon dating puts some of the excavated material at an astonishing nine thousand years old, which would place the citadels four and a half thousand years before Mesopotamia, the oldest known civilization. While sea-bed finds are notoriously tricky to assign to a definite place of origin, as they may have been shifted by the ocean over time, such dates could connect the destruction of Krishna's fabulous coastal capital with the worldwide rise of seawater following the end of the last ice age. This in turn could tie in with the great flood stories that are found in Indian scriptures, just as they are in other ancient cultures all over the world.

Draw a diagonal line south-east from Dwarka across the subcontinent and you strike Chennai. Drive fifty minutes further south and you come to the little coastal town of Mahabalipuram. Once an unvisited fishing village, this picturesque spot is the site of several spectacular rock cut temples and caves dating from the 6th – 8th centuries AD, and is nowadays firmly on the tourist circuit. We know these works of art belong to the time when Mahabalipuram was the main port of the mighty Pallavas, a maritime dynasty that ruled over much of south India and took armies, trade and Indian culture far into south-east Asia. But local legend has it that long before the Pallavas arrived, the giant king Bali built his sumptuous capital here, hence the name Mahabalipuram which means 'the city (*puram*) of the great (*maha*) Bali'. So magnificent was the place that the gods became jealous, and they sent the sea to destroy it. It is said the bells from the drowned city's temples can still be heard from far out under the waves on the nights of full moon festivals. Another romantic myth, this oriental Dunwich?

Well, not to the local fisherman who have for generations been snagging their nets on underwater protuberances far out to sea off the present coast. And, once again, recent marine archeological investigations have indeed revealed the presence of a group of man-made structures on the ocean bed some three miles offshore. Are they the remains of Bali's ancient capital that, like Krishna's Dwarka, was submerged by the rise of the oceans resulting from what religion described as divine anger and science calls the end of the ice age?

Continue on further south along the coast from Mahabalipuram and you will reach the temple town of Rameshvaram, a bustling pilgrimage spot perched on the south-eastern tip of the subcontinent. The place is held to be holy because it was from here that the dramatic *dénouement* of the Ramayana epic unfolded. For Rameshvaram was the site of the bridge that Lord Rama, assisted by armies of monkeys and bears, built across to Sri Lanka to rescue his wife Sita, who had been kidnapped and imprisoned by the island's demon king Ravana. Long dismissed as a construction of arcane poetic fantasy, this bridge has looked much more of a reality following recent NASA photographs from space. These revealed underwater remains that prompted research uncovering traces of an ancient and clearly man-made structure intermittently connecting coastal Tamil Nadu to Shri Lanka. It follows the exact course of where the epic tells us the bridge ran.

NASA satellite photography has also shed light on another long-running historical puzzle that lies at the heart of our understanding not only of the unfolding of civilisation in the subcontinent, but across the entire ancient world. The pre-Hindu settlers known as the Aryan (or Vedic) people are generally believed to have entered the subcontinent about 1,800 BC, forcibly overrunning the Indus Valley Culture which, since about 3,000 BC had been settled along the banks of the great river Indus that flows through what is now Pakistan. Vedic scriptures say little about the Indus, but wax lyrical about what they called 'the mightiest river in the world'. This was the Saraswati, that 'flowed from the mountains to the sea' and along which their people settled. They hymned the Saraswati as a life-giving goddess, but no such river remains today.

Yet another imaginative myth? So assumed all the academic experts until recent satellite imaging revealed the subterranean course of a river bed that, before it dried up some six thousand years ago, had indeed run right across north India from the Himalayas to the Gujarat coast. This followed the course of the Saraswati as described by Vedic texts, and it was indeed mighty, being over twenty kilometers wide in places. Moreover, along its banks lie the remains of a huge number of settlements of the supposedly pre-Aryan Indus Valley people. The anomalies raised by these discoveries may end up turning our current ideas of ancient history on their head. The Vedic people, believed to have entered India about 1,800 BC, describe a river that dried up well over two thousand years before that date. This river was populated by extensive settlements belonging to a civilisation the Vedic people were supposed to have destroyed. Was then the IVC not destroyed by the warlike Aryans? Did it survive to live harmoniously side by side with the newcomers? Or were they even different parts of one united culture that flourished for many millennia across much of north India between the subcontinent's two great river valleys?

That this last scenario may be the right one is being suggested by an increasing number of scholars, particularly those who, unlike their predecessors, have not just accepted the received wisdom but have actually read the Vedic texts in the original Sanskrit and attempted to correlate those accounts with recent scientific and archeological evidence. Indeed, the received wisdom has long been shown to be deeply flawed supposition. Very few skeletons indicating a violent death have been found in the hundred and fifty-odd IVC sites that have been uncovered, and those that do have been shown to have come from different strata and therefore belong to widely different times. So the long-held idea of an Aryan invasion, the theory popularized by the British archeologist Mortimer Wheeler in the 1930's, when the idea of warlike Aryans looking for *lebensraum* was very much in the European air, looks untenable today. The best survey of the latest state of play is to be found in *In Search of the Cradle of Civilisation*, by D. Frawley, S. Kak and G. Fuerstein. It makes a recondite subject fascinating.

Time scales of the ancient world are being revised all the time, and India is no exception. In early 2011 it was announced that stone axes and cleavers found near Chennai put tool-using humans in India 1.5 million years ago, which is long before such an evolutionary stage was reached in Europe and about a million years earlier than previously thought. Another re-think concerns India's role in global interconnectivity. Pattanam in Kerala boasts India's greatest yield of Roman amphorae — jars used for wine, oil and fish sauce — and a well preserved canoe. The jars number over 1000, and many of them came from Catalonia, probably being transported by merchants from Alexandria via the Nile and then the Red Sea sometime in the first three centuries of the Christian era. Further up the coast, the seabed off Mumbai has also recently yielded many Roman artefacts, including stone anchors, from the 5th – 6th centuries AD, showing trade flourished between Rome and India several hundred years later than previously thought.

Sadly, in the wake of the 2008 seaborne terrorist attacks in Mumbai all submarine archeology off India's coasts is currently suspended. It seems we shall have to wait a little longer to enjoy the next expansion of the frontiers of knowledge that are continually being extended by the fruitful interaction of science, history and 'myth'.

27

Never the twain?

RUDYARD KIPLING WAS for many years something of an embarrassment to the liberal literary establishment, perceived as the jingoistic voice of the British Empire no-one wanted to hear. In fact, Kipling is a writer of much greater subtlety, intelligence and compassion than he is usually credited. Unconvinced? For a start, try reading his novel *Kim* again. If you want evidence of his common touch, remember *If* is consistently voted its favourite poem by the British public. His gift of empathy? You'll find it with the British Tommy in the *Barrack Room Ballads* poems and with children of all ages in *The Jungle Books* and the *Just So Stories*. Then go on to his highly relevant morality tale of greed and its consequences: *The Man Who Would be King*. This short story was made into a wonderful film by John Huston in 1975, with a stellar cast: Michael Caine, Christopher Plummer, Sean Connery and Saeed Jaffrey. It also featured an all too brief appearance by the stunning Shakira Caine as an Indian princess. Highly recommended.

But the strong stuff is Kipling's war poetry. As is so much of his work, the poems are shot through with ambiguity, evincing a protective outer skin of patriotism shredded by his enduring grief at the pointless death of his only son, aged eighteen, in some forgotten Flanders field. The boy had been disqualified for military service because of poor eyesight; disappointed, his father in effect smuggled him through the recruiting process so he could pass the minimum regulations. Just imagine the twisting knife of regret. Some of his verse gives a hint:

> 'Our statecraft, our learning,
> Delivered them bound to the pit and alive to the burning
> Whither they mirthfully hastened as jostling for honor.
> Not since her birth has our Earth seen such worth loosed upon her!
>
> *… But who shall return us our children?'*

In the aftermath Kipling was asked to write a history of his son's regiment, the Irish Guards. It took him five and a half years, and produced what is considered not only a superb military history but a literary masterpiece. He called it "my great work...done with agony and bloody sweat".

Much better known of course is Kipling's most famous line: 'East is East, and West is West, and never the twain shall meet' but most people are unaware that his point was to emphasise that such differences are in no way absolute, as long as we are mature enough to look beyond them to our common humanity. The poem's next lines, which nobody ever includes in the quote, neatly turn their predecessor on its head:

'But there is neither East nor West, Border, nor Breed, nor Birth,
When two strong men stand face to face, tho' they come from the ends of
the earth!'

Such open-mindedness ran counter to the spirit of his times, and though the tone may sound dated, the sentiment is still pretty good.

Two rather impressive blends of East and West have recently hit the headlines. One is Indian–American rocket scientist, K.R. Sridhar. This young boffin has invented the 'Bloom Box', a unit filled with a new type of fuel cell that generates electricity cheaply and cleanly and, unlike sun or wind power, is dependable 24/7. Downtown office blocks and Indian villages would benefit alike. A spin–off from NASA technology developed for the exploration of Mars, Sridhar's units are small, cheap to make and provide unmatched efficiency. When run on fossil fuels they are almost 70% cleaner than existing coal-fired systems, when run on renewable sources, 100% cleaner. Interviewed recently, Sridhar said "We believe we can have the same kind of impact on energy as the mobile phone had on communication." Wow.

The other is William Bissell, son of a Punjabi mother and American father and the boss of Fabindia. By taking traditional Indian dress and tweaking it with contemporary style, fabric and colour, this outfit has cleverly managed to satisfy both the Indian middle class's need for cultural roots and its voracious hunger for the new. A whole range of lifestyle goods followed. The result? A global brand that has grown twenty five-fold in the last seven years.

As can be seen from the extraordinary success of his company, Bissell is no utopian dreamer. Nor is he a friend of clumsy central regulation. All the clothes, food, toiletries and furniture Fabindia sells so successfully are produced by small-scale local cooperatives in a sustainable way; only the marketing and distribution are in centralized hands. These worker co-operatives operate at village, small town and city levels as inclusive and integrated production outfits that owe more to Gandhi's far-sightedness than World Bank myopia.

But Bissell's interests stretch far further than the interiors of middle-class Delhi or Mumbai. He has a vision to restructure the Indian economy and make it an example for the 21st century world. Bissell's main insight is that third world development based on Western-style consumerism is just no longer viable — think resources and pollution. A taste of his many revolutionary ideas: (1) a reassessment of assets, whereby the poor living in asset-rich land — clean water, forests, fertile land — could trade these against goods and commodities produced by asset-poor cities (2) factoring the hidden cost of environmental degradation into all consumer goods and (3) setting up exchanges to facilitate recycling/disposal between manufacturer and consumer, so that from its outset the life of a product is environmentally managed. There are dozens more such ideas, set out in practical detail in his fascinating book *Making India Work*.

2011 posted the highest ever annual increase in global carbon emissions (up 5.9 % from 2010) and India is the second largest atmospheric polluter after China, sending 1.5 billion tons of CO_2 into the atmosphere each year. These facts, combined with the global financial crisis, present the governments of the world with an opportunity to move the global economy away from its current high-emissions trajectory. Men like Bissell sound like indispensable advisors in this situation; let's hope his insights are not too bold, or just too common-sensical, to scare off the ruling forces of government inertia and commercial vested interest.

Oh, and by the way, William Bissell should meet K.R. Sridhar — standing face to face of course.

28

Nothing is ever lost

IT IS BELIEVED in India that the last thought at the time of death is the expression of the inner nature of one's mind. As such, it is an important influence on the direction the soul takes after death. It is therefore recommended that the dying person should focus their mind on the thought of their favourite deity or their *guru*, and thus create a positive image to help guide the soul in its passage through the realms of the afterlife and into its eventual rebirth in a new body. This belief also accounts for the universal practice of reading the scriptures to the dying. In addition, it is held in Hinduism, as in all the great faiths, that no spiritual work is ever wasted, because God is working out all our individual destinies through the instrumentality of whatever circumstances and events are necessary. These two weighty ideas come together nicely in the following folk story.

There was once a man who did penance all his life in fervent worship of the great god Shiva. But nothing seemed to come of it, and as he lay dying he thought miserably to himself, "What was the point of all my effort? I have got nowhere. Despite all my worldly success, all I really wanted was to meet Lord Shiva, and I never did". He duly died and was eventually reborn as a bee, no longer burdened by thoughts of Lord Shiva, his rituals or his penances. But nothing that has been gained spiritually is ever lost; at the very depth of his mind lingered the desire to reach his Lord.

One day this bee flew to the holy city of Varanasi, unaware in his new form that the ancient pilgrimage site on the banks of the holy river Ganges is the place on earth where the mighty Shiva is said to reside. As he entered the city, the bee was drawn by the beautiful scent of flowers into the garden of a rich merchant. He surveyed the scene with delight, and before long, climbed into one of the blooms, intent on drinking its luscious nectar. So absorbed was he in his enjoyment that he quite lost track of time, and when night fell — suddenly, as it always does in the Orient — the flower closed up and trapped him in its silken embrace.

Early next morning the merchant came into the dew-laden garden to pluck some flowers to use in the morning worship of his chosen deity, who happened to be Lord Shiva. Being a devout man he took care to seek out only the choicest and most scented blooms. As fate would have it, among the flowers he picked was the one containing the bee. Carrying it carefully inside along with the others, the man duly offered it in *puja* to the image of his god. After the ceremony, as the offered flowers lay in front of the image, the warm rays of the rising sun fell on them and their petals slowly opened up. The bee crawled sleepily out.

Lord Shiva was delighted to see him, exclaiming: "Oho! So here comes one who as a man worships me fruitlessly for so many years and then takes the form of a humble bee to get even closer to me!" As a reward for such devotion, Shiva offered the bee the boon of whatever he wished. The bee asked to be eternally united with his Lord. And so he was.

29

Oh, Kolkata!

IF HE HADN'T been cremated, Jyoti Basu would be turning in his grave. For those who don't know, Basu, who died in 2010 aged 96, was the man who came within a whisker of becoming India's first ever Communist Prime Minister. The son of a middle-class doctor, he was educated at one of the best Catholic schools in Calcutta. As a student he indulged in transgressive capers such as breaking into the city's poshest whites-only club with some friends and splashing noisily around in the swimming pool until they were hauled out and forcibly ejected. The young man then went to London, and once there followed in the footsteps of three revolutionaries who had also honed their ideas in the capital of the Empire. Like Gandhi he studied law; like Lenin and Marx he discovered his vocation to be Communism. Back in Calcutta Basu soon became a pillar of the anti-establishment, eventually winning office as West Bengal's chief minister. Somehow he managed to survive the chaos of 1967 when Maoist violence brought down his government and martial law was imposed. Ten years later he was back in the chief minister's chair and remained ensconced there until 2000.

A typical Bengali — intelligent, proud, independent-minded — the grand old man of the Indian left would surely be horrified at the recently announced plans of his successor. For Mamata Bannerjee, the current chief minister, has a scheme to paint Government buildings, flyovers, roadside railings and taxis a shade of light blue. Ms. Banerjee has decided that the theme colour of the city will be sky-blue because the motto of her new government is 'the sky is the limit'. "Blue is a beautiful colour and is also soothing for the eyes," purrs her mayor Sobhan Chatterjee. Basu would certainly have preferred bright red — a suitably unsoothing revolutionary colour that would have blended well with Kolkota's age-old worship of the blood-drinking goddess Kali. She gave her name to the place after all, and she still receives sacrifice of he-goats each Tuesday and Saturday at her temple by the river. But even more galling to the old freedom fighter than Ms. Bannerjee's choice of pigment would surely be the fact that after ousting the left to gain office in mid-2011, she lost no time in announcing that the new crew was planning to 'convert Kolkata into another London'.

The city already has its own St. Paul's Cathedral and a Victoria Memorial Museum; their story, and much more, is told in Geoffrey Moorhouse's excellent book *Calcutta*. But now a six-mile stretch of the Hooghly River is planned to become the South Bank of West Bengal. There will be a 'Calcutta Eye' wheel, allowing dizzying city-centre views and Curzon Park, named after the former Viceroy, will become a public space of 'Hyde Park standards'. Alipore Zoo, originally a collection of exotic animals assembled by a Governor-General of Bengal called Richard Wellesley, (brother of the Duke of Wellington) is now to be refashioned after the zoo in Regent's Park. And a Calcutta School of Economics will offer LSE type degrees awarded by London University. Fortunately, no one has yet had the bad taste to mention the scandal of a few years back when a Calcutta University student bought some nuts off a stall in the street and found they were wrapped in one of his exam papers that had been sold, unread and unmarked, to the nut *wallah*.

Ms. Bannerjee has her work cut out to upgrade the city's image. Long before Mother Theresa reconfirmed it as a black hole, the place had a lousy reputation. Founded by a Londoner called Job Charnock in 1680 as a warehouse for the East India company, by 1750 Calcutta was known as Golgotha, 'the Place of Skulls', because so many died there. A sea captain called Alexander Hamilton who sailed the eastern coast at this time tells us that out of 1,200 Englishmen alive at the company warehouse one August, 400 were buried by the following New Year's Day. The worst decade was 1747–57, when 74% of EIC employees there died.

The atmospheric Park Street cemetery is not part of the planned revamp, but its worn and mildewed tombstones bear eloquent testimony to the evanescence of early colonial life. It was said that if you survived two monsoons you would be alright. The reaper's sickle was grimly democratic; even winning high office was no protection. In one eight year period, three Governor Generals and two of their wives died from disease, whilst from 1822–31 no less than four Bishops of Calcutta perished. The city's problem was her low-lying and swampy hinterland, the perfect breeding-ground for every sort of bug. Malaria and cholera were its regular annual exports, bubonic plague a more occasional one. But not that occasional. By the end of the nineteenth century, the Russians had established the 'Quarantine Cordon', a line of manned posts along the Afghan-Persian border primed to intercept EIC trade caravans and ensure that they were not carrying the plague into the motherland.

In defence of Mother Kali's hometown, it should be added that a significant contributor to the death toll among ex-pats was their gross dietary habits. Many Europeans in India simply ate and drank too much for a climate which did not tolerate an imported gastronomic culture whose bulging girth encompassed many daily jugs of beer, claret and gin on top of those gargantuan Victorian breakfasts. It may well have been safer to drink alcohol than water in the first city of the Empire, just as it was in contemporary London, but over-indulgence often proved fatal.

Low-lying Calcutta was supplanted by higher and drier Delhi as the capital of British India in 1911, by which time the swampy city, always politically literate, was already buzzing feverishly with the idea of independence from the Raj. A few years earlier, in more optimistic times, the then viceroy Lord Curzon had written:

> 'a glance at the buildings in the town, at the river and the uproar and the smoke, is sufficient to show that Calcutta is a European city set down on Asian soil'.

And that, in an ironically post-modern sort of way, is just what Basu's native place now seems set to demonstrate. The haughty English aristocrat would certainly have approved of Ms. Bannerjee's refurbishment scheme. The wily Bengali communist? I doubt it.

30
One coin

A BRACE OF tales nicely illustrates the great paradox of human existence: set against the eternal cosmic vastness we are fragile, evanescent and totally insignificant specks and yet, simultaneously, each one of us is unique and infinitely precious.

The mighty Indra, king of the gods, once determined to have a new palace. He wanted it to be the most splendid building ever seen, and so he hired Vishvakarma, the patron deity of all craftsmen and a being of great wisdom, to be the chief architect. Work went on for months, and gradually a fantastic building came up, more splendid than anything ever seen before. Eventually it was finished, and the day the astrologers deemed auspicious for the grand opening ceremony arrived. All the gods and goddesses had been invited to attend, and tremendous work had gone into making the festivities suitably magnificent.

When the sumptuous affair began, Indra was seated on his throne at one end of the great hall of public audience, raised up on a dais above the assembled gathering, with Vishvakarma occupying the seat of honour at his right hand. In the middle of a long and rather tedious congratulatory speech from one of the guests, Vishvakarma suddenly began to giggle. First surprised, then offended by such frivolity, Indra turned to him, demanding sharply:

"And just what is so funny as to make you interrupt such an important and solemn occasion?"

"I do apologise your Majesty" replied the architect "But I have just noticed those ants". So saying he pointed to a long line of ants that stretched from one of the plates of sweetmeats that covered the banquet table all the way back across the hall to the doorway. "So, there are some ants" replied Indra gruffly "what of it?"

"Well, your Majesty" came the reply "it is just that each and every one of those ants has already been an Indra in the past, or is destined to become an Indra in the future"

The king of the gods lowered his head and said nothing.

The second story concerns a squirrel. Lord Rama and his army of righteousness were stationed at Rameshvaram, preparing to rescue Sita from the demon-king Ravana who had imprisoned her in his island fortress of Lanka. While the bridge was being built there, it was the monkeys and the bears that shouldered most of the responsibility; the cleverness of the one and the great strength of the other formed a powerful combination. But actually all of Nature was combining in the great enterprise; all the seen and unseen forces united to restore the rule of *dharma* in that evil age.

Many an evening Lord Rama liked to disguise himself and wander among his people, listening unobserved to their concerns and learning at first-hand what they were feeling. One such evening as he moved quietly through the ranks of his followers, he noticed a little squirrel hopping along towards the bridge with a pebble clutched tightly in her paws. Reaching the great heap of boulders she carefully deposited her stone. Some of the monkeys saw this and began to jeer cruelly at her, saying that such a small pebble was a waste of time and only those stalwarts, like themselves, who could bring big heavy rocks were of any use in building the bridge.

Lord Rama stepped forward. Throwing back his shawl to reveal his identity, he bent low and carefully picked up the squirrel. Cradling her lovingly, he addressed the monkeys:

"Oh no, not at all! Do not make the mistake of thinking that this little squirrel's contribution is worthless. She has acted in good faith and done everything in her power, and that is what matters. Who can say what the end result of any action may be? All we can do is do our best and retain balance of mind, whatever the apparent outcome. This is real devotion, and she has shown it. So rest assured, however humble her contribution may appear, it is every bit as important in the long run as anything that you are doing."

So saying, he tenderly stroked the little creature. And that is how, my best beloveds, the squirrel got those five cream-coloured stripes along its back — they are the mark of Lord Rama's fingers.

31

One mania, one vote.

IN TIMES PAST, it was accepted without question that belief in God was a good thing. Nowadays, such an automatic acceptance is no longer afforded to the Almighty, but it does seem to have been transferred to the concept of 'democracy'. The 'D' word is our modern Absolute, unquestioningly assumed to be unquestionable, a noble and progressive cause, an inalienable right, even. Well, alright, but the trouble with such shibboleths is that they always seem to be etched in blood by the wrong hands, and their inarguably necessary defence all too often involves going off to war all over the place and the consequent slaughter of thousands of innocents.

In India, democracy has been around in some form for a long time. The system is mentioned in hoary Sanskrit texts: the grammarian Panini (c. 650 BC) describes independent and self-governing federations (*jatas*), and there are records from 550 BC onwards of democratic Buddhist assemblies (*sanghas*) which persisted in some areas for a thousand years. It was perhaps these that Diodorus, an historian accompanying Alexander the Great's abortive excursion into India in 326 BC, cited as the 'democratic republics' he found to be flourishing in the sub-continent.

But the great and the good have not unanimously supported the tyranny of the majority. Socrates decried it as being 'full of variety and disorder' and for Plato the only just form of government was an aristocracy under those wise enough to disdain money and power, the philosopher-kings. An astute modern observer of politics, Gore Vidal, classicist that he was, would have been very well aware who he was echoing when he remarked "Any American who is prepared to run for president should automatically by definition be disqualified from ever doing so."

Some say democracy is a façade masking the reality of rule by hidden elites, inevitable because only elites possess drive and initiative, whereas the masses are divided and apathetic. Others champion monarchy, arguing a king would always want to bequeath his descendents a stable inheritance, while a short-term career politician is only out for himself. More to the contemporary point perhaps, is economic guru Milton

Friedman's belief that democracy's inherent discontinuity renders it irrelevant in a developing country where stable rule, economic growth and reduction of poverty are the priorities. Anyway, he adds, even in developed countries, voters are chronically irrational, biased and uninformed. Fair point there, Milton.

In the midst of the economic turmoil swirling around as 2011 staggered to a close, the European Bank for Reconstruction and Development noted a sharp drop in popular support for democracy in the countries that joined the EU after the fall of the Berlin Wall. Those on the borders of that troubled institution seem likewise inclined. Austria's Freedom Party, and Finland's True Finns are both doing well with their anti-immigration and authoritarian policies, and these are rich countries whose economy has held up fairly well. Hungary, also outside the EU but suffering severely from its large scale borrowing there, provides a starker outlook. One of its major parties, Jobbik, is accused of being racist and wielding a paramilitary arm yet continues to gain increasing support, but it is Fidesz, which won an overwhelming parliamentary majority last year (democratically) that is really raising political eyebrows. Clever manipulation of the system, including much old-fashioned gerrymandering, looks like establishing the party in an almost unassailable position. Judicial independence is being compromised as the courts are stuffed with party loyalists; moves are being made to muzzle the free media and a proposed constitutional amendment would effectively criminalise the leading left opposition party. And now in Greece, the dysfunctional mother of European democracy that has consistently voted for policies that have brought the country to the very brink of bankrupcy, the fiercely anti-immigration Golden Dawn party comes marching over the horizon, with its rousing slogan: 'Burn the Brothel called Parliament'. All over Europe alarmists are muttering darkly about the 1930's.

Meanwhile, half-way across the world, its largest democracy can always be relied upon to produce a sort of lunatic entertainment with scandals that make even Italian politics look well-behaved. Recently two stories originally released by Wikileaks to The Hindu, the respected left-leaning English language daily, have gripped the nation. One tells of how, in 2008, opposition parties tabled a motion of no-confidence in the ruling Congress-led coalition government. Apparently, 'in order to win the no-confidence motion, Rs. 50 to 60 crore, was paid to a number of MP's'. Following this bribe, (a whopping £7 to 8.5 million sterling), 19 opposition members duly about-turned and voted with the government. An official from the US embassy was shown the chest full of cash; Indian tv aired footage of bundles of notes being thrown around the chamber. Leftist leaders excoriated such 'gross moral degeneration and crass political opportunism'.

But it wasn't long before the left was itself embarrassed by another notes for votes scandal. This time those standing squarely in the dock were Tamil Nadu's Dravidian left-populist party, the DMK and its offshoot the AIADMK, founded in the 1970's by the matinee idol M.G.Ramachandran and long since presided over by his sometime mistress, the current chief minister of Tamil Nadu, iron lady Jayalalitha. The story also features Frederick J. Kaplan, acting Principal of the US Consulate General in Chennai, who described what he called a 'sophisticated operation' to distribute cash to bribe voters. "Weeks before the elections, agents of the parties come to the neighbourhood with cash carried in rice sacks. They have copies of the voter lists and they distribute money based on who is on the list. The agents come in the middle of the night, between 3 and 4 am when the Election Commission is asleep." (Erm, call that sophisticated, Fred?) Elsewhere, the DMK distributed money to everyone on the electoral roll in envelopes inserted in their morning newspaper, along with voting slips detailing who to vote for.

One forthcoming politician named Oswaisi obligingly informed the jaw-slackened Kaplan that donations to constituents — e.g. paying off a marriage bill, digging a well, funding a medical operation — were always sympathetically considered before elections. When asked if such things weren't illegal, Oswaisi cheerfully replied "Of course, but that's the great thing about democracy!"

Oh Plato, thou must be turning in thy grave!

32

Outsourcing holy horse-power

EVERYONE KNOWS that India is the world capital of outsourcing, and though China's rates are more competitive, her lack of English is so far holding her back. But now there is a new twist to the story: the subcontinent is providing not just material services but spiritual ones as well. While the West suffers a growing decline in all things religious, India, with no shortage of sacred technicians, is stepping into the gap and offering high-quality, low-cost spiritual help.

The outsourcing of holy horse-power began here in Kerala, the capital of the Catholic Church in India. Kerala's six million Catholics, living predominantly in the central part of the state, make up about 20% of her population. The West's disillusion with Rome, beginning with doctrinal disputes in the 1960's and rocketing with all the recent child abuse scandals, has led to an acute shortage of priestly recruitment and with it those available to perform both intercessory prayers, said on behalf of others, and special masses. Step forward God's Own Country. Prayers for others and masses for a special purpose, known as 'mass intentions', have always been part of orthodox Catholicism, but global hi-tech now makes such things quicker, easier and cheaper. For some Kerala priests 'mass intentions' have become a valuable source of income, though church authorities here are quick to stress that the overwhelming amount of transubstantiation taking place among the coconut palms is for the benefit of native Indian believers.

Christians are not the only beneficiaries of hi-tech good vibes. In Sikhism, the main communal rite is the *akhanda path* or 'unbroken recitation' of their holy book, the Guru Granth Sahib. This is a collection of hymns, prayers and poems by Kabir, the poet-saint who inspired Sikhism, and the succession of ten *gurus* who then organised and led the faith. Indian tv has a channel dedicated to broadcasting the *akhanda path* from the Sikh sacred capital, the Golden Temple in Amritsar, and very beautiful it is too. An *akhanda path* can be commissioned to overcome a specific problem or gain general help in life. In the West, a 48 hour recitation by a rota of professional singers will set the faithful back $1000; in a temple (*gurudwara*) in the Sikh homeland of the Punjab, it is a tenth of the price.

Hindus too are getting in on the sacred act. There are several websites offering *puja* — ceremonies worshipping the gods — which are performed in temples in India for very competitive rates, starting at a few pounds and going up to several hundred. The aim of these *pujas* can range from increasing one's wealth to finding a good spouse or overcoming a black magic curse. Simple fire offerings called *havans* or *homas*, and their more elaborate versions known as *yagyas*, are also available. A full blown *yagya* — the rite dates back to the beginnings of civilisation in the subcontinent — can involve dozens of officiating priests, hundreds of offerings into the sacrificial fire and can go on for days on end. Depending on its scale, a *yagya* can cost up to thousands of pounds. All these fire rituals are performed to secure worldly and material benefits, though the altruistic can also commission them for general wellbeing, such as communal harmony or world peace. In Orissa recently, over 100 Vedic priests performed a yagya to Laxmi, goddess of wealth, to tackle the global economic slowdown that has now also hit the subcontinent.

It is not just Indians who are employing these remote spiritual services, which include huge numbers of horoscope readings. A website called puja-by-choice.com says it handles requests from 26 countries around the world and only one in ten of its clients is a non-resident Indian. And surprisingly, among those who are NRI's, many are young. The site adds that they understandably prefer these ceremonies to be done in their homeland as they feel the purity of having proper priestly *brahmins* officiate in the traditional way will add to the power of the ritual.

Outsourced sacred technology is definitely a growing market. And now, with *The Best Exotic Marigold Hotel*, so is unwanted old age. As so often, Indian ingenuity is filling a gap and satisfying a need that others are unable or unwilling to.

Jai Hind!

33

Remember Akbar's finger

YOU ARE TRAPPED in the throes of some personal melodrama and a well-meaning friend offers the consoling balm: "Well, you know, things always work out for the best in the end". Grrr! Platitude or truism, the sentiment is universal and ancient, no doubt persisting because it bestows a needed sense of order and meaning to what would otherwise be the random and chaotic nature of human experience. In India it dovetails nicely with the teaching on *karma*, which states that everything we experience is the entirely appropriate consequence of a previous action.

The Mughal Emperor Akbar the Great was roughly contemporary with Elizabeth 1st of England, and probably the greatest of India's rulers: just, tolerant and blessed with an insatiable curiosity about the world. His life and its context can be found in Bamber Gascoigne's *The Great Mughals*, which is beautifully illustrated too. Akbar was unschooled and illiterate, but he was a great patron of learning and surrounded himself with a brilliant cabinet, the so-called 'Nine Jewels'. The most sparkling of these was his Prime Minister, Birbal. Stories about Birbal's wit are still recounted in the villages as if he lived only yesterday. Here is one of them.

One day Akbar's finger badly bitten by a hawk he had just acquired. The wound didn't heal in the damp monsoon weather, days passed, eventually his physician reluctantly recommended amputation to forestall gangrene. Recovering from the operation, Akbar fell into a depression. Birbal tried to lift his spirits. "Well your Majesty" he said: "You know these things work out for the best in the end". Infuriated by such an inane observation, the Emperor had Birbal thrown into a pit to teach him a lesson. Galvanised by his anger, Akbar decided to cheer himself up with his favourite pastime: hunting. Accompanied by a few servants, he set off into a dense forest after tigers. Whilst there, they were ambushed by a gang of *thugees**, roaming brigands who worshipped Kali, the bloodthirsty Goddess of Destruction. Their leader immediately recognised Akbar, and was delighted that he had the opportunity to offer such a sacrifice to the Goddess. Surely She would grant him anything he wished after receiving the head of the most important man in the land? Preparations

---

* hence the English word 'thug'. John Masters' novel *Night Runners of Bengal* is a good read on the subject.

were duly made, but at the last moment, the sacrificial priest noticed that Akbar was missing a finger. To offer anything damaged or deformed is an insult to the deity, and so the Emperor was released as unsuitable. The leader of the *thugees* touched the royal feet, apologized profusely and sent the relieved party on its way.

Returning to the palace, Akbar was in a joyous mood. He went straight to the pit in which Birbal was confined and ordered his release. Later, the two sat on a terrace drinking wine together. "Well, Birbal" laughed the Emperor, "I have to admit that this time your counsel about things working out for the best was true: that wretched amputation actually saved my life! But mark well, it is not an infallible principle. In your case it resulted in your spending a couple of days cooped up in a stinking pit!"

Birbal smiled diffidently. "I beg to differ, your Majesty. If I had not been in that pit, I would have accompanied you as usual on the hunt. Seeing you lack a finger, those *thugees* would have turned to me. Although of much lesser stature than your royal self, as your chief minister I would nevertheless have been deemed an acceptable offering to the Goddess". Not for the first time, the Emperor lowered his head in acknowledgement of his favourite minister's sagacity.

So, the next time you feel like throttling that well-intentioned friend, remember Akbar's finger. Perhaps things really *do* work out for the best...

34

Some linguistic records

EVERYONE LOVES TO set and break records, but as a glance through The Guinness Book shows, Indians specialize in bizarre ones. Traveling to all 194 countries of the world in the shortest recorded time, (six years, 10 months and seven days) and suffering the world's longest industrial tribunal (12 years) are just a couple of them. Several others feature human sproutings: Sawan Singh has grown the world's longest beard (2.36 metres), Sridhar Chillal boasts the longest fingernails (6.15 metres) while maestro coiffeur Jawed Habib briefly became something of a national hero, winning his place in the record book by setting 410 hair styles in a single day. Well, now there is a new Indian record: one Job Pottas recently took only one minute and 40 seconds to spell 50 words backwards, thereby knocking a whopping 40 seconds off the previous fastest time.

As a Keralite, Mr. Pottas speaks Malayalam. This is the only language whose name is itself a palindrome and it is a tongue of both fiendish difficulty and mellifluous charm. Moreover Malayalam is spoken at such breakneck speed that one wonders if Malayalis have the knack of breathing through their ears, or gills perhaps. But of course Indians have always had a way with language. The government recognises 22 major ones — each as different from its neighbour as are those of Europe — and hundreds of minor ones, with countless local variant dialects. Many Indians will speak three or four of the major tongues in addition to the *lingua franca* English. One recent prime minister, the liberalising economist Narasimha Rao, spoke no less than 17 languages, and fluently.

And then there is Sanskrit, that most perfect of ancient tongues. The West learnt of Sanskrit thanks to William Jones, a Welshman and one of the most brilliant minds in an age of unparalleled intellectual virtuosity. A fiery advocate of universal suffrage, political rights and popular education and a friend of Benjamin Franklin, he was lauded as 'the most enlightened of the sons of men' by Dr. Johnson, a man not remembered for tossing compliments around. At Oxford Jones read law, but his passion was teaching himself languages. By the time he died he was fluent in thirteen and familiar with over two dozen more.

The erudite young man came to India as a judge in the High Court of Calcutta; while there he threw himself into a profound study of the country and its culture, founding the Asiatic Society of Bengal and voraciously examining every aspect of Indian intellectual life: chronology, law, music, chess. A vegetarian who lived simply and kept cows, he was fascinated by the zoological and botanical life he saw around him and produced unsurpassed records of India's plants and trees. The ashoka tree commonly seen in north India today is named *ashoka jonesiana* after him.

But most of all Jones loved Sanskrit, which he studied with orthodox *brahmin* pundits and mastered without effort. They accepted him as a reincarnation of one of their own — an astonishing tribute from the most conservative caste of India's intelligentsia to an officer of the occupying British Raj. In 1786 Jones wrote:

'The Sanskrit language, whatever be its antiquity, is of a wonderful structure; more perfect than the Latin, more copious than the Greek; and more exquisitely refined than either; yet bearing to them both a stronger affinity than could possibly have been produced by accident; so strong indeed that no philologer could examine all three without believing all three to have sprung from some common source which perhaps no longer exists'.

Jones' discovery showed that languages fall into families that share common grammatical forms. Thus Sanskrit and its derivatives in north India (Hindi, Bengali, Punjabi etc) belong to the same 'Indo-European' family as Greek, Latin, and the Romance, Celtic and Germanic tongues and their off-shoots. And Sanskrit, while not being the direct parent of them all, is certainly the oldest known relative in the family, as Jones' praise infers. Moreover, within any one family, one language can be used to shed light on another, so the discovery of this ancient priestly tongue provided something of a rosetta stone that gave rise to the modern science of comparative linguistics. Scientists, ethnologists and historians were compelled radically to revise not only their theories on the origins and classification of language, but all the then prevailing notions of human and cultural evolution. It was a landmark achievement in a remarkable life; he died at the early age of forty-seven yet who today remembers the brilliant William Jones?

Given the Welsh genius' unjust fate, the fame of Job Pottas seems unlikely to outlive him. But his son Geordie should and the lad appears to be following in his father's footsteps. Currently studying law, he can pinpoint the exact number of letters in a word, sentence or paragraph in record time. This unusual talent has already won him a place in the Indian Book of Records. Ah, it must be in the seneg (5)!

35

Sound horn and trust God

THOSE UNFAMILIAR WITH the subcontinent sometimes wonder if Indians drive on the left or the right. The answer, of course, is neither: they drive in the middle. I remember a dramatic example. I was on tour somewhere, sitting, as usual, in the front right-hand seat. (Old traveller's tip: this is the safest place, as it is directly behind the driver who, in an emergency, will always instinctively steer to save himself). Another bus was bearing down from the opposite direction, straight towards us. I waited for the usual last-minute swerve ... it didn't come. I really thought that this was the end, my own personal Kalki had arrived, horn blaring to sound the trump of doom. Then, at the last nanosecond, the oncoming bus did finally swerve, but not quickly enough to avoid clipping off our wing-mirror with a sharp crack. As the vehicle flashed past, I turned around, fully expecting to see it over-correct and career off the road into the ditch. Somehow, it didn't, but corrected its over-correction and lurched manically on down the road. I then noticed there was a dishevelled sadhu standing by the roadside. Our wing-mirror had fallen right at his feet. He calmly bent down, picked it up, and began adjusting his matted locks in it as if nothing had happened. Later, thinking about the incident, I remembered the belief that an advanced yogi has such a powerful thought force that his desires are spontaneously satisfied without his having to make any effort.

Some people assume that the way Indians drive indicates they are terrible drivers, but the opposite is the case. Indians are fantastically skilled drivers. How else could they leave things to the last moment, squeeze through gaps by fractions of an inch, drive for such long, hot hours without losing concentration and have the endless patience to put up with the traffic jams and queues and groaning bullock-cart roads without going berserk? But they don't. Road-rage is a very rare occurrence in India, and a bump with another car rarely elicits more than a rueful grin or a brief mock display of indignation. There is none of the tight lipped insurance stand-off such an incident would provoke in Europe; generally speaking driving in India is a mellow drama rather than a melodrama. All the same, the question remains, why do Indians chose to drive in the way they do?

To applaud India's driving skills is not to say that all is well on her roads, as a glance at their verges will confirm, as do the official accident figures. These are chilling. At least 13 people die every hour in road accidents here, making an annual toll of well over 100,000. Of these, Kerala, which is not the worst state, accounts for about 3,400, (i.e. roughly as many fatalities as in the UK). An awful lot of those can be attributed to the private bus companies that ply National Highway 17 as it snakes down the west coast from Goa in the north to Trivandrum in the south. These juggernauts are insanely competitive. The first to reach a stop gets to pick up the waiting passengers, so they literally race each other to keep to the absurdly tight schedules the companies enforce on them. The result? Open a newspaper almost any day and you will find grisly stories of buses ploughing off the road, crashing into bus shelters or shops, hurtling headlong into one another or crushing other innocent vehicles to sardine cans. Frequently, the reports tell us, the driver 'absconds', chased by 'an irate mob'. People are fed up with the situation, now and then there's a half-hearted campaign to get automatic speed limiters fitted on the buses, but nothing ever gets done and the mass-murderers of NH17 continue to wreak havoc. All for the sake of saving a few minutes. There should be roadside hoardings all over Kerala displaying Gandhi's wonderful saying: 'There is more to life than increasing its speed'. But then of course the buses would be driving too fast to read them.

Given that her accident figures are so sobering, it is strange that many of India's drivers drink. But they do, the professional ones that is: truckers and haulage men. Punjabis have the worst reputation. Red Bull, the amphetamine syrup that lubricates the transport industry in Thailand is expensive in India, so the preferred stimulant here is usually what the Indians call 'spurious liquor' i.e. local hooch. In Rajasthan, opium is used. For the desperate, boot polish spread thinly on a *chapatti* is said to do the trick. But let's look on the bright side. Just imagine the mayhem if Indians weren't such good drivers!

Beware of generalisations. I have had dozens of drivers in India who were models of restraint and sobriety. Piety, even. On one occasion at a stop somewhere in Uttar Pradesh the kitchens, not realising my driver was a life-long vegetarian for religious reasons, served him a curry containing meat. With a palate no doubt dulled by tiredness and hunger he tucked in, but it did not take long for the horrible truth to dawn. Those unacquainted with Indian dietary mores may find it hard to imagine the depth of mortification such an occasion could cause. My hostess was also very upset. She immediately provided him with enough money so that, the minute his assignment with me was over, he could take the train up to the sacred city of Haridwar and ritually purify himself in the holy Ganges from the consequences of his unwitting error.

Speed and drink and whatever else aside, the rising accident figures are not only due to the increasing number of the vehicles on the road, but also to their type. For several decades after 1947, unless you were a Maharajah with a Rolls, there was effectively only one Indian car: the iconic Ambassador. This Indian-made version of the Morris Oxford (series III) that first emerged gleaming from the famous Cowley factory circa 1958, fitted well with the egalitarian aspirations of the newly independent country. If you were one of the relatively few wealthy enough to have a car, you had the same car as everyone else equally privileged — be they prime minister, businessman, senior civil servant or whoever. It was not quite Henry Ford though, as there was a choice of black or white.

There have been few variations made to the king of the Indian roads since that time because this stately mechanised sofa was supremely well-suited to the road conditions here. Being only moderately speedy, it did not pose undue danger to the ox-carts, pedestrians, cattle and elephants it shared the roads with; being sturdy, it was tough enough to deal with some appalling road surfaces and, being solid and heavy it afforded its passengers good protection in the event of a crash. And it was mechanical, and therefore cheap and easy to repair. If you broke down in some remote area, someone would appear from the nearest village, crawl under the car with only a ball of wire and a pair of rusty pliers and somehow the thing got fixed. If a headlight went, you just unscrewed the bulb and fitted a new one — no fussing around with costly and sealed electronic units in those days.

The stately Ambassador can even be seen tootling around London today: for the last ten years a fleet of them have comprised Karma Kars, a taxi service based in Notting Hill and created by ex-hippie and self-styled lifestyle guru Tobias Moss. Tobias' website quotes the Taoist axiom that 'the journey is more important than the arrival'. Now, this may sound a potentially disastrous philosophy for a taxi company, but at least each of his cars is individually and lovingly kitted out: bumpers are festooned with brightly coloured flowers, ceilings set with mirrors, seats covered with glitzy Indian fabrics and dashboards deified by a Ganesh. I know of no better car for that special occasion.

The Ambassador gracefully surrendered her near-monopoly, and a new chapter was opened in Indian motoring history, with the introduction of Japanese models, particularly the Maruti, in the 1980's. This both precipitated, and coincided with, many more Indians becoming car owners. Travel liberation transformed life for millions, as it always does, but the effects of such rapid and unbridled change in motoring habits without any adequate planning were dire. Look at Bangalore; the former 'garden city' was once a place of wide, tree-lined boulevards and a widely-envied climate, now it is a nightmare of pollution and gridlock. In fact it is so bad that the IT locusts are deserting it in swarms, ravenously moving on to Hyderabad now and next, so it is rumoured, to Mangalore.

Early 2009 saw the launch of 'the peoples' car' the Tata Nano which, at about £1300, is the world's cheapest. The advent of this tiny rear-engined run-around is a powerful social symbol, much as were the Model T, the VW Beetle and the Mini in their time. But in those days there was space, affordable fuel, fresh air, no global warming and many, many less people. As a relative latecomer to mass car-ownership, India faces a huge challenge in how best to handle the motoring aspirations of her upwardly and horizontally mobile millions. Rigorous planning is required, but India doesn't really do rigorous planning. Perhaps an optimistic pointer to the future is the way Delhi has drastically cut down on pollution in the last few years. In all public transport diesel has been replaced by concentrated natural gas, and many private cars are also using CNG. As a result the air quality in the city has improved hugely.

The new cars are light, fast and fragile, one consequence of which is particularly evident in the mountains. Holidaymakers from Jalandar, Gurgaon or Delhi scoot up to resorts such as Shimla or Mussoorie for the week-end, have a few drinks, drive too fast and sail spectacularly off the edge of twisting unfenced roads to land up a couple of thousand feet below. The crumpled carcasses of Marutis, Fiestas and Suzukis can be spotted all over the foothills.

Scariness apart, one of the pleasures these mountain roads afford the driver is their roadside gallery of signs. You are treated to a unique literary sub-genre, boldly executed in the ever-charming language of Indinglish. Most messages manage a rhyme, and some are direct: *'Driving faster can cause disaster' 'Three enemies of road: liquor, speed and overload', or 'Peep peep, don't sleep'*. As this is India, many have overtones of religion: *'Keep your eyes on the road, otherwise it will take you to heavenly abode*', the supernatural: *'Not witchcraft but watch craft that saves lives'* or Gandhian philosophy: *'Simplicity is the peak of civilisation'*. Some are rather daringly addressed to young bloods: *'Darling I like you, but not so fast'*, *'Be gentle on my curves'* or *'Love thy neighbour, but not while driving'*. Others are clearly for the domestically settled, and can be either realistic: *'Darling, do not nag me as I am driving, instead turn your head and enjoy the nature charming'*; dramatic: *'If you sleep, your family will weep'*, or starkly cinematic: *'Traffic jam, yellow tape, parent crying'*. One of my favourites is this sage advice for the unpredictable journey of life: *'Be courteous to those you meet on the way up, you may meet them on the way down'*. And some, like much Indinglish, need a double-take before the intended point is grasped: *'Please drive slowly, safety fast'*.

India is now well and truly part of the modern auto world, with Mercedes, Lexuses and BMW's increasingly common, smoked glass windows and all. Her Formula 1 track, with one of the longest straights in the world, was inaugurated outside Delhi in the Autumn of 2011, courtesy of the efforts of liquor baron Vijay Mallya. Peugot-Citroen has just announced plans to build a $1 billion plant in Gujarat that will churn out 170,000 cars a year by 2014. The news will come as a blow to Tamil Nadu as the two states are battling it out to become the Detroit of India. The area around Chennai already has BMW, Ford and Renault-Nissan factories and tops the league of car exports, but her poor infrastructure — frequent power cuts, heavily congested roads and sometimes chaotic port facilities — as well as her distance from the big centres of Mumbai and Delhi, are making foreign investors wary. Overall, annual car sales are predicted to reach 5 million by 2015.

Stuck in the evermore inevitable traffic jam, any driver here has ample opportunity to contemplate the future of his country's roads. His desire to do something about it is surely doomed to remain frustrated, but at least he can avail himself of what is perhaps, after all, the best advice available to Indian drivers. It is the slogan cheerfully proclaimed from the back of the lorry in front of him: Sound Horn and Trust God.

36

Stop telegrams Stop

THOSE OF US ancient enough to remember telegrams — so exciting to receive and curiously empowering to send — will sympathise with Indians today. In news not widely telegraphed, India has discontinued its international telegram service. Formerly the humming crown of a countrywide nervous system, The Central Telegraph Office in Delhi is no longer a busy place. In the good old days it served hundreds an hour, but now you can count its customers on the once busily tapping fingers of one hand. A list of suggested standard greetings still hangs on the wall however, ranging from Number 1 which offers "Heartiest Diwali Greetings" to Number 43b: "I Pray at the Feet of Maharaja Shri Agrasen for the Success of the Program Organized". Hmm, useful, that one.

The telegram would have succumbed to electronic communication long since if not for government policy to keep it humming in those areas where the internet has not yet penetrated. Its other saviour was a quirk of Indian law, whereby telegram receipt is proof admissible in court that a document has been sent, whereas emails are not. In a country so trussed up in the red tape of endless legal entanglements, such proof is vital. Curiously, the fact that telegrams are put into a computer and then sent by e-mail to the receiving office where they are printed out and posted, in no way reduces their value as evidence. The company responsible for the system, Bharat Sanchar Nigam, is evasive on how many telegrams it handles. Its website claims there are 121 telegraph offices in India but notes that it is 'a diminishing service'.

So then, the end of an era. It is a cruel irony that a technology that celebrated unprecedented speed is to be condemned to such a lingering death. Its pioneer in India was William Brooke O'Shaughnessy, a doctor who also introduced Western medicine to the benefits of cannabis. Its effects didn't seem to dull his practicality: he won official approval for his communications work after setting up a demonstration line between central Calcutta and a suburb 27 miles away called Diamond Harbour then, as now, the daily market for the city's favourite gastronomic delicacy: *hilsa* fish. His patron, the Governor-General Lord Dalhousie, took up the cause with such enthusiasm that over the next four years more than 3,000 miles of wires were strung all across the country in one of the Raj's many extraordinary feats of engineering in the subcontinent. The first real test of the system came all too soon: telegraph operatives were able to alert British authorities across the country to the rapidly spreading uprisings of 1857, variously known as the Indian Mutiny, the Sepoy Revolt or the First War of Independence, according to your perspective. Sir John Lawrence, then commander of the army in the Punjab, famously exclaimed: "The telegraph has saved India."

Telegrams were also used by the Raj to celebrate an aristocratic love of classical learning long gone in our more narrowly educated times. When General Napier captured the province of Sindh from its Muslim rulers in 1843, he notified England with all the panache of a Boy's Own Paper hero. His telegram contained just one word: *Peccavi* — Latin for 'I have sinned'. (Those who do not appreciate puns may have to read this twice). There was another military commander, Sir Colin Campbell, who lacked the dash which won Britain so many victories in India, but was regarded as a brave soldier and a prudent leader. His soldiers were devoted to him, though enemies who disliked his overly cautious style nick-named him 'Sir Crawling Camel'. But there was nothing slow about his wit. When he relieved the siege of Lucknow in November 1857 Campbell upstaged Napier — his own classical telegram home proclaimed: *Nunc fortuna habeo* meaning: 'I have luck now'.

Well, times have changed, and luck now seems to have deserted India's extensive telegram service. One of many results will be the consigning of such witty international japes to history Stop

37

Successful Sikh seeks successor

AT THE BEGINNING of the 17th century, the newly-formed religion of Sikhism, in many ways a fusion of Hinduism and Islam, came under increasing attack from its hostile Muslim neighbours. After the fourth Sikh leader, Guru Arjun Dev, was murdered on the orders of the Mughal emperor, his son Guru Hargobind set out to militarise the Sikh nation. Men were instructed to carry arms, including the iron bracelet (*kara*) and small blade (*kirpan*); hair was worn long and wrapped around the head in a turban to protect the skull and make every Sikh man instantly recognisable. Hargobind also set up schools to train a warrior group called the *Akali Nihang*, 'the Immortal Crocodiles' to be a military elite skilled in the martial art known as *shastar vidya* 'the science of weapons'. Today the Nihangs are still a fierce bunch. They can be seen particularly in rural Punjab, always wearing blue and often travelling in groups on horseback, armed with swords, spears, muskets and sometimes more modern weapons. Nihangs follow their own Hinduised version of Sikhism and, like itinerant Hindu *sadhus*, many take *bhang*, an infusion of cannabis, to get closer to God.

Initially influential, the Nihangs became steadily marginalised. Their status suffered a body blow when Maharaja Ranjit Singh, the one-eyed 'Lion of the Punjab' chose to by-pass the blue clad warriors and hire ex-Napoleonic army officers to train the army he was assembling to fight against the British and establish the Punjab as an autonomy Sikh state. The French input didn't help much; the Sikhs were finally defeated in the second Anglo-Sikh War in 1849, and forced to give up arms and any hope of independence. The Nihangs suffered the weight of British retribution. According to contemporary military accounts, Raj troops were ordered to open fire on any man with a blue turban and a weapon.

So it is a nice irony that the fate of *shastar vidya* now rests in the hands of a British Sikh. A former food-packer and father of four from Wolverhampton, 44-year-old Nidar Singh is thought to be the only remaining master of the martial art. He is now engaged in a full-time search for a successor. Until he was 17, Nidar wore his hair short and dressed like any other British teenager. He was largely ignorant of his

Sikh heritage and knew nothing about martial arts, though he was a keen wrestler. But a trip to see an auntie in the Punjab changed all that. While there, he met Baba Mohinder Singh, the 80 year old hermit who became his guru. "When he saw my physique he looked straight at me, and even though I was clean-shaven, asked: "Do you want to learn how to fight?"" says Nidar. "I couldn't say no."

On the first day of training, the frail old man handed the youth a stick and instructed him to hit him. When he tried, the master "threw me around like a rag doll. I just couldn't touch him," Nidar recalls. "That definitely impressed me." So he spent the next 11 years on his auntie's farm; in the mornings he milked the buffalos and for the rest of the day he trained with his guru.

In 1995 Nidar returned to Britain, married and got a job in a factory. But his real passion and purpose was teaching *shastar vidya* and immersing himself in research on early Sikh military history. His attempts to revive a culture and practice that left the mainstream more than 150 years ago have caused some animosity within the British Sikh community. In his first two years as a teacher he received more than eighty death threats from those who disagreed with the ideology of *shastar vidya* and dislike the beliefs of the Nihangs he identifies with. Undeterred by such gadflies, Nidar currently spends a lot of his time researching the art in India and Pakistan, searching for descendents of the Akali Nihang tradition and adding to his vast collection of weapons. As supporters of traditional culture, we at The Hermitage heartily wish the intrepid two-eyed 'Lion of the Midlands' the best of luck in his efforts!

38

That'll do ricely!

INDIAN mathematicians of old were highly inventive people. They gave the world the concept of zero, the decimal point and our so-called Arabic numerals (brought to Europe from India by the Arabs) — all of which revolutionised scientific thinking and practical life. To take but one example: the financing of the European Renaissance was greatly facilitated by Italian merchants being able to dispense with cumbersome Roman numerals and calculate interest using percentages.

History does not record the name of one astute Indian mathematician, the man who invented that most mathematical of games, chess. When he had finalized the prototype set he presented it to his local Maharajah, who was so delighted with the game that he offered it's inventor any recompense he wished: jewels, elephants, gold and so on. The man smiled shyly and produced a single grain of rice from his pocket. Placing the rice grain on a corner square of the chessboard, he humbly requested that the number of grains be doubled on each successive square — two on the second square, four on the third, eight on the fourth and so on. That simple gift would be sufficient recompense from such a mighty monarch. The king was surprised that a man intelligent enough to invent chess should be so stupid as to want only a few heaps of rice in recompense, but, happy that he could get away with such a niggardly gift, quickly agreed. He was to regret it. By the time the sixty-fourth square had been reached, the inventor had so much rice that not only could he could sell off a tiny portion for a fortune, but by planting and in a few months harvesting the remainder, he and his family were secured as the wealthiest persons in the kingdom from then on.

How so? Well, for mathematicians, the answer is simple: the accumulative power of 1+2 E 63. The rest of us, unable to get our heads around the implications of this equation, need only know it resulted in 8 billion billion grains of rice, which, it has been calculated, would have filled a warehouse with a 25 x 25 km footprint and a height of 100 metres. Check-mate, your Majesty!

I do not know whether the little heap of rice that lies on Hanif Kureishi's table is descended from the wily chessman's hoard. I suppose it must be. Hanif, his table and his rice are to be found most days outside the main gate of the splendid Indo-Saracenic pile in downtown Bombay that is officially named the Chhatrapati Shivaji Maharaj Vastu Sangrahalaya but which everyone mercifully still calls the Prince of Wales Museum. This Harif Kureishi is not related to the well-known and somewhat controversial British author of the same name, but he is a writer, and in his own way, possesses a skill no less unique than does the *enfant terrible* of post-colonial literature. Bombay Hanif is not interested in the sexual and familial imbroglios that his London namesake finds so fascinating, in fact his literary pretensions could hardly be less complicated. For a few rupees he will simply write your name and a smiley face or a heart, or a longer message, or anything you want really, up to a total of 300 letters — 'alphabets' as he calls them — all on a single grain of rice. He does not wear glasses and uses no visible means of magnification, just holds the grain with tweezers in one remarkably steady hand and a tiny brush loaded with paint in the other. The rice is standard basmati, the paint acrylic, the result astonishing. To put it in perspective: 300 letters is well over two tweets. Not yet thirty, Hanif has been scribing his rice grains for ten years or more. The finished product is slipped carefully into a little phial filled with a preserving medium of jasmine scented hair-oil (he used to use coconut oil but it clouded when cool) which he then attaches to a key-ring. This deft little routine brings him a lot of money, especially on festival days when the crowds that troop dutifully around the museum are delighted by his nonchalant dexterity.

Hanif is a modern practitioner of an ancient art, as painted rice grains have long been good luck charms in the Orient where rice symbolises abundance and prosperity. The Turks are said to have been its most skilled miniaturists; their oldest examples lie in the Topkapi Palace museum in Istanbul. Over the millennia scribes have transmitted civilization by embellishing clay, papyrus, animal bones and skins, tree bark, leaves and paper. I like the fact that in the age of the plasma screen someone can still earn a good living by writing on rice. In his humble way Hanif is no less a master of the painstaking art of the minute than those ancient Indian mathematicians and their decimal points.

39

The Princes and the British

UNTIL THEY WERE persuaded to join the Indian Union in 1947, the Maharajahs ruled over a third of the subcontinent and a quarter of her population. The stories about these remarkable rulers are legion and by far the best collection is the classic work: *Lives of the Indian Princes*, by Charles Allen and Sharada Dwivedi. No one who reads or writes about the Maharajahs can avoid this book; much of what follows is certainly indebted to it.

The East India Company's gradual growth of power throughout the eighteenth and early nineteenth centuries owed much to these 'native princes', who granted the rights to trade and hold land, and following the Crown's assumption of government after the events of 1857 (which the Raj called the Indian Mutiny and the Indians the First War of Independence) the Maharajahs constituted what was effectively a second tier to her Majesty's government. This arrangement suited the British well since it removed much of the burden of attempting to govern an enormous and diversified land that had inexorably absorbed every foreign ruler that had tried to impose its will on her. Paradoxically, the autonomy of the Maharajah's was in no way been diminished after the Mutiny, as this brief but bloody conflict had shown Britain very sharply the impossibility of attempting to rule the whole country by force. So the Raj was happy to let the princes enjoy their autonomy as long as they acknowledged the ultimate authority of the Queen Empress, paid their taxes and referred the highest legal questions to the relevant officers of the governing authority. In effect the Maharajahs acted as a largely autonomous bulwark between the British and all those subjects who were not under direct rule of the Crown, a role very similar to the one they had played under the Mughal dynasty that preceded the British.

Princely loyalty to the Raj took more tangible forms than mere acquiescence, however, especially in the military sphere. In both the World Wars, Maharajahs voluntarily offered the allied war effort their private armies — raised, equipped and maintained entirely at their own expense — and sometimes distinguished themselves on the field of battle. The camel corps led by the Maharajah of Bikaner in Rajasthan fought for Britain in both world wars, seeing active service in France, Palestine,

Egypt, Burma and even China. Gwalior sent infantry and hospital ships to help the British in the first War, and it was the Jodhpur Lancers that led the assault on Haifa in General Allenby's Palestine campaign in 1917. At one point, when the battle looked hopeless, the Maharajah's cavalry halted as if to retreat. It is said that he offered his troops a stark choice. "You can go forward and be killed by the enemy's bullets or you can fall back and be executed by me". They advanced, and Haifa was won from the Turks.

Jodhpur is perhaps better known for the riding breeches named after him. On the way to Victoria's Diamond Jubilee celebrations in London, his luggage somehow got lost at sea, and the prince was reluctantly forced to reveal the secret of how his favourite trousers were made to a Saville Row tailor. In the second War, Jaipur was one of the leaders of the crucial assault on Monte Casino in Italy in 1943, and Bundi won the Military Cross for his part in the Burma campaign.

While the Maharajah of Benares was the spiritual head of the Indian princes, due to presiding over the most sacred city in Northern India, the senior figure in the secular hierarchy was the Maharana of Mewar — modern Udaipur. He was the head of all the Rajputs, the ancient military aristocracy known as the *kshatriya* or warrior caste. It was the proud boast of the house of Mewar that it had never demeaned itself by alliance with any foreign ruler. This spirit continued under the British, being best exemplified in modern times by the redoubtable Maharana Fateh Singh (b. 1853). In 1903, when the power and self-confidence of the Raj was at its height in the subcontinent, the then Viceroy, Lord Curzon, held a *durbar* in Delhi. Fateh Singh, while always friendly and respectful, could not honourably allow himself to attend the event. It is said he went as far as the railway station in Udaipur, then turned back making some excuse. The next *durbar*, in 1911, saw another gilded and embossed invitation. This time a chair beside their imperial majesties King George 5th and Queen Mary was set aside for him. Another refusal; today the unoccupied chair is proudly displayed in Udaipur's City Palace museum.

Fateh Singh was one of the very few princes who refused to support the British war effort. As he said: "When there is a fight in India, Europeans don't come here to die, so why should we send our Indians to die when Europeans fight?" Nevertheless, after the war he was awarded the Empire's highest military honour — Grand Commander of the Star of India an order founded to reward those Indian princes who had stood loyal to the Raj during the uprisings of 1857. Fateh Singh looked at the medal lying in its velvet-lined case and commented acidly to his interpreter "This is the sort of bauble attendants wear. Put it on the horse; it looks better on a horse than on a King". Showing the sort of diplomacy that no doubt kept him in his job, the interpreter explained to the British emissary that as it was not an auspicious day, his Majesty would don the medal on a more suitable occasion. Later, when someone asked the Maharana what he had done to be awarded such an honour for doing nothing, he responded "On the contrary, I rendered the British the highest service. While they were away fighting in Europe, I refrained from taking over Delhi. Isn't that service enough?" British Political Agents were frequently put in their place by the ruler; one Resident asked for a map of the state and was presented with a poppadom, with the explanation that its wrinkles gave as accurate a picture of Mewar territory as any map.

But Fateh Singh did have his uses for the British. Once he urgently summoned the British Residency Surgeon from Ajmer, in the north of Rajasthan, as his son and heir had acute appendicitis. A fleet of the swiftest racing camels travelled all night, reached Ajmer and returned to Udaipur bearing the breathless surgeon. He operated immediately, using a table set up in the main hall of the palace with all the women of the household assembled to watch from the balcony above. The doctor was so nervous at holding the life of the son and heir of the senior Indian prince in his hands that he compulsively whistled 'Mary had a little lamb' throughout the operation. After it was successfully completed, the surgeon was again sent for; this time he had to whistle the whole tune over again whilst it was recorded onto one of those early cylindrical discs that preceded the gramophone. The disc was carefully wrapped in velvet and kept as part of the Udaipur royal treasure as the magical *mantra* that had helped save the life of Fateh Singh's son.

Although the occasional Maharajah was known to be despotic, debauched or even demented (the Nawab of Jeora was regularly advised by a panel of six courtiers drawn from the ranks of the local lunatic asylum) it was the unwritten convention that what a ruler did under his own roof was his own business, particularly in the large states whose power and funds earned them full autonomy. The British did not always get on with the native princes — for example they had continuously hostile relations with the Holkar royal family of Indore and would have liked to depose them but could never find the suitable pretext.

Only one ruler behaved in such a way that a section of his own people took up arms against him, and that was Jay Singh of Alwar. According to one Political Officer who knew him, Alwar was a man 'sinister beyond belief'. The prince saw himself rather differently, as a reincarnation of the god Rama, in fact. He liked to sport a hat that he swore was the replica of one he wore in his previous deified existence. More easily verified is the fact that he is the only person ever to have delivered a speech to a group of British MP's in Sanskrit. As was widely known, he could speak perfect English. When asked the reason he explained that when the English came to India they spoke their own language, "so when I come to England I shall speak mine".

Alwar's ability to charm the then Secretary of State for India enabled him to remain on the throne far longer than he should have, but the British authorities eventually decided that his rampant debauchery rendered him unfit to govern. The final straw was allegedly an incident involving a good-looking young Englishman, a mahogany dining table and a pair of automated handcuffs. Indians have always enjoyed mechanical toys, which have regularly played their role in the noble arts of both love and war. The best-known example is surely 'Tippoo's Tiger', a barrel organ disguised as a tiger that has for years been relentlessly mauling a near life-size European soldier in the genteel environs of South Kensington's Victoria and Albert Museum. It was made in the 1790's for Tipu Sultan 'the Tiger of Mysore' by a French firm (the French were Britain's great rival in India at the time) and its bellows were designed capable of generating both the tiger's roars and the soldier's shrieks. The acme of ingenious machinery in the service of love was probably the bed made for the Nawab of Bahawalpur in 1880. It was fashioned of rosewood generously encrusted with 290 kilos of silver, and at each of its four corners stood a life-sized statue of a voluptuous woman — exemplifying the fair sex of, in turn: France, Greece, Spain and Italy. The figures were bronze but painted in flesh tones, sported wigs made of human hair and, through clever mechanics, were capable of winking at the occupants of the bed while waggling the horse hair fly-whisks and fans they carried. The bed was also fitted with a music box which, when a button under the mattress was pressed, played a 30-minute interlude from Gounod's opera 'Faust'.

Alwar's mechanical device was altogether more diabolical. It consisted of a heavy silver table centre-piece whose carvings concealing a hidden pair of automated manacles that sprang shut when the ornament was pressed. One evening, his unsuspecting dinner guest, the aforementioned good-looking young Englishman, was invited to lean over the table and admire the workmanship of the centre-piece by placing his hands on it. In a trice he was trapped, held fast and rendered vulnerable, thus allowing the lascivious Maharajah to do with him exactly as he pleased.

Jay Singh was deposed in 1933, and sent into exile in France where he died four years later. Yet in some way he had the last laugh. It was the custom in Alwar for the body of a deceased ruler to be carried to the cremation ground in procession. So the Maharajah was embalmed and his body brought back to India where, dressed in full regalia, it was levered into the state car for its last journey. Just as the funeral procession was starting, one of the princes decided that it would be more fitting if his father's closed eyes were covered with dark glasses. The effect was so lifelike that people lining the route began to wail and fall on the ground; a rumour rapidly spread that the erstwhile ruler was to be burnt alive as this was the only way to exorcise his wickedness.

Many of the Maharajahs sought to cement their English connection through education, preferably in Britain but otherwise at one of the boarding schools set up in India along the lines of a British public school. These, such as St. Paul's in Darjeeling, were frequently in the Himalayan foothills where the Raj presence was already strong due to it's custom of moving up each year to escape the oppressive heat of the plains. Others, such as Mayo College at Ajmer or Aitchison College in Lahore, were sited near important army bases.

Another way to gain the prized educational passport to the wider world was to employ a British tutor. This custom spawned a curious little literary genre, of which the best examples are *The Hill of Devi* by E.M.Forster and *Hindoo Holiday* by J.R.Ackerley. Both books are written-up diaries recounting the time their author spent as a private tutor to a minor Maharajah; both writers were gentlemen temperamentally attuned to enjoy the camp intrigues that often lurked beneath the bejewelled and silken surface of palace life, and both have bequeathed us a very amusing read laced with some acute observations about Indian life that still ring true to this day.

Colonisers seem to take alcohol with them — the Greeks, Romans and American pioneers certainly did — and one habit the Maharajahs picked up from the British was drinking. Some of them become extremely good at it. India traditionally preferred stimulants ranging from the mildly intoxicating sherbets imported from Persia by the Mughals as a substitute for alcohol, to the various decoctions of hashish known as *bhang*, a drink still widely enjoyed. Opium, though it could be smoked or eaten, was more usually taken in liquid form, a communal practice that continues nowadays in some areas of Rajasthan such as when the former ruler socialises with the headmen of his villages. Some drinks were reserved for royalty, such as the aphrodisiac liquors called *ashas*, which could contain fifty or more strange ingredients ranging from human blood to crushed gemstones.

While those princes who became Europeanised playboys tended to hang out in the louche ambience of Cannes or Monte Carlo, those who enjoyed sport spent time in Britain. An example of the latter was Maharajah Jam Sahib Ranjitsinhji of Nawanagar. As a young man in the 1890's he overcame racial prejudice to play first class cricket for Cambridge University and then test cricket for England. His performances at county level for Sussex were particularly fine (in the 1900 season he averaged 87), in fact 'Ranji' as he was popularly known, was one of the sweetest strikers of the ball of all time. His unorthodox technique and rapid reactions brought new flair to the game — the 'leg glance' is one of several strokes attributed to him. Other princes also excelled at this most English pastime which dovetails so well with the Indian character. The Nawab of Pataudi and the rulers of Baroda, Porbander and Dungapur were particularly celebrated.

Another accomplished sportsman who enjoyed being in England was the polo-loving Maharajah Man Singh of Jaipur, whose team thrashed everyone it played against, whether in India or England. 'Jai', as he was known, was the husband of the impossibly beautiful Gayatri Devi, who died in 2011. She liked to be known as Ayesha, after the autocratic heroine of H. Rider Haggard's novel *She (who must be obeyed)*. Her autobiography: *A Princess Remembers* gives a good feel of her world. In the early 1970's, when the royal families were finally losing the long-running battle with the Congress party to preserve their privy purses, Ayesha was thrown in jail by her arch-enemy Indira Gandhi because she refused to reveal the hiding-place of the legendary Jaipur jewels. Accumulated when the royal family was close to the Mughal court — Akbar the Great married a Jaipuri princess — they were said to be second only to those owned by the Nizam of Hyderabad, then the richest man in the world. In happier times long before his wife's imprisonment, Jai used to visit England regularly to play polo, and acquired Saint Hill Manor, a fine 18th century sandstone pile in East Grinstead, as a convenient base for games at nearby Cowdray Park. It was after a fall from his horse there that he died in 1970. By then he had already sold Saint Hill to L. Ron Hubbard, the Svengali of

Scientology, and it remains the European headquarters of that curious organisation today.

It was the royal family of Punjab that had the strongest connections with Britain, which is ironic as that state was the only one in recent history to fight against the Raj for its independence. The man who lead his people in the Anglo-Sikh Wars was Maharajah Ranjit Singh, the one-eyed 'Lion of the Punjab'. His youngest son, Duleep Singh, was born into this political turmoil in 1837 and at the age of five proclaimed Maharajah. Following the defeat of the Khalsa Army in 1846, the treaty of Lahore gave the British Government responsibility for the administration of the state and the protection of the boy sovereign. Duleep's kingdom was reduced by half and a British Resident installed in Lahore. Three years later the twelve year old Maharajah was deposed and made to sign over the sovereignty of the Punjab and relinquish all claims to the property of his kingdom and much of his personal fortune. This included the Kohinoor diamond, which the then Governor General Lord Dalhousie passed on to Victoria who swiftly added it to her crown jewels. The boy was exiled to the southern periphery of his former kingdom, to a place called Fatehghar which by rights should merit the adjective 'God-forsaken' but for the fact it was an energetic centre of Christian missionary activity in Northern India. While there Duleep duly embraced the 'one true faith', but if British officials felt that this conversion had finally emasculated the son and heir of Ranjit Singh, they were sorely mistaken. However, it would take many years for the young prince to show his true colours.

A year later Duleep set sail for England, quickly gaining a royal audience with Victoria, who immediately took to him, as she did to several of her young Indian subjects. She is reported to have written of the young prince that "Those eyes and those teeth are too beautiful" and she was to become godmother to several of his children. Duleep was a frequent visitor to the Palace, and the Queen also invited him to stay with the Royal Family at Osborne, where she sketched him playing with her children and Prince Albert photographed him, while the court artist Winterhalter made his portrait. Throughout his teens and into his twenties the young prince lived in Scotland, not far from Balmoral. He was known as The Black Prince of Perthshire and enjoyed an admiring reputation due to the lavishness of the receptions, shoots and entertainments he hosted.

In 1860 Duleep returned to India to rescue his mother from political exile in Nepal, and received an enthusiastic welcome from his excourtiers and Sikh soldiers. Three years later he was there again to consign his mother's ashes in the Ganges, this time bringing back a wife who was part-Ethiopian, part-German and thanks to an upbringing in a Cairo mission school, spoke Arabic. Together this exotic couple moved to rural Norfolk, where they must have created quite a stir. Their home was Elveden, near Thetford, selected and purchased for him by the India Office, and they set about transforming the run-down estate and rebuilding the church, workers' cottages and local school. The house became a semi-oriental palace with walls like a *shish mahal* 'palace of mirrors' and huge paintings of Ranjit Singh holding court at the Sikh Golden Temple. The Prince of Wales was a regular guest on shoots.

But despite an English education, adopted religion and the life-style of a European royal, the rebellious Sikh spirit had not died. Renouncing Christianity and re-initiated into Sikhism, Duleep decided to return to India as the prophesied leader of the Sikh people. He didn't get very far. Arrested at Aden he returned to Europe, but soon established clandestine contacts with supporters in the Punjab, Irish home-rulers and Russian revolutionaries. He issued a proclamation claiming to be 'the lawful sovereign of the Sikh nation' but destiny willed it otherwise. His health broke down and while staying alone in the Hotel de la Tremouille in Paris he suffered a fatal epileptic fit, allegedly brought on by the belated realisation that his second wife was a spy planted to monitor his activities. Contemporary reports speak of his 'dark and mournful end' in the autumn of 1893. His wish for his body to be returned to India was not honoured. The authorities feared such a symbolic gesture might provoke unrest in a country increasingly resentful of British rule so Duleep was buried with Christian rites and under the supervision of the India Office in Elveden Church. His wife and one of his sons lie there with him. In 1999 a bronze equestrian statue was unveiled by the current Prince of Wales in Thetford, in memory of the Sikh prince's generosity to the town.

The family line came to a somewhat inglorious end. Duleep's eldest son Victor got off to a terrifically British start — Eton, Trinity, Sandhurst and then the Dragoons — but he soon went to the bad. While serving in America he won the affections of the daughter of a wealthy New York banker and their engagement was announced, but ugly rumours of his profligacy and gambling debts had already begun to surface, so daddy soon put an end to that little caper. On the death of his own father Victor became head of the Royal House of the Punjab, and four years later as Prince Victor Albert Jay Duleep Singh, he married the daughter of the Earl of Coventry, a friend from his Cambridge days. She was eight years younger and the mixed marriage created quite a sensation, but disapproving gossip was calmed by the intervention of the Prince of Wales and the wedding took place at what was then London's most fashionable church, St Peter's in Eaton Square. But only four years later and despite his annual income of $45,000, Prince Victor was declared bankrupt with debts to the tune of half a million dollars. The gambling addiction plagued him for the rest of his life; he spent most of his time in Europe and died in Monte Carlo in 1918, aged only 51. He was buried in the Anglican Cemetery that overlooks the town, from where his soul could gaze down on the casinos where his body had lost so much of its cash. Perhaps Prince Victor was consoled when his wife was laid to rest beside him but in death as in life, Lady Luck continued to toy with him, as he had to wait for another thirty-eight years.

Let us end on a happier note, and one that also involves regal gambling. It concerns Indira Devi, the Maharani of Cooch Behar and mother of the aforementioned Gayatri Devi of Jaipur, said to be the most beautiful woman in the world. Indira herself was stunning, as contemporary photos show, and she had an inimitable sense of style. Visiting Le Touquet in the 1920's, she drew all eyes one evening when she descended like a vision on the casino, wearing a gorgeous sari of brilliant silk emblazoned with emeralds, rubies and pearls. The Maharani was a winner that night, but a large pile of chips was not the only thing beside her at the table. There was also a small turtle, its shell set with three lines of jewels — diamonds, emeralds and rubies — that was her lucky charm. One English observer, a Mrs. Evelyn Walsh, described the scene: "Every now and then the creature would crawl across the table but every time she caught it back. The crowd was totally mesmerized by her". No wonder.

40
The real thing?

NEXT TIME YOU knock back a Coke here in Kerala, spare a thought for the inhabitants of Plachimada. Never heard of the place? You are not alone. But a few years ago this little village in the Palakkad district of the state did hit the headlines. Why? Cue the world's favourite sugar fizz and environmental pollution. It's been a long-running saga. In the most recent episode, a high-level government committee, headed by Chief Secretary K. Jayakumar, (a personable character who is a writer, poet and Malayalam film lyricist in his spare time) submitted a damning report claiming damages against Coca Cola. Its demand was a whopping Rs. 216 crores (about £30 million) in compensation for the environmental and human damage caused by the drink giant's Plachimada bottling plant .

The first observed problem was the lack of local water. Over-extraction had lowered the water table so much that the village women were having to leave paid work to spend much of their day scouting for potable water. Emergency tankers were organized by the local council to ship water in, and they have been operating ever since.

Then came evidence that wells and other water-bodies were polluted, followed by contamination of the surrounding soil. This was thanks to industrial effluent, a heady cocktail of cadmium, lead and chromium, in the form of a toxic sludge that the company initially recommended to local farmers as 'manure'. Local agricultural production — vegetables, meat, milk and eggs — suffered drastically. And last in the chain came human health and well-being: widespread skin ailments, respiratory problems and low birth weights have been recorded, while resultant economic disruption, school dropouts and lost career opportunities are also claimed. Coke rejects the report, commenting: "It is unfortunate that the committee in Kerala was appointed on the unproven assumption that damage was caused, and that it was caused by Hindustan Coca Cola Beverages". Try telling that to the inhabitants of Plachimada.

No doubt this one will continue to run. Don't forget this is the country that suffered the world's worst industrial accident, the Bhopal gas tragedy, which the government in 2006 stated had caused 10,000 deaths and well over half a million injuries with lasting effects, mainly cancers and liver failure. There is also continuing pollution of the Bhopal environment. Over a quarter of a century after the event victims are still seeking compensation from Union Carbide and Dow Chemicals and still trying to get the Indian authorities to come up with effective health treatment programmes. On the 27th anniversary of the blast many of them began an 'indefinite' campaign to stop trains passing through the city of Bhopal by sitting down on the tracks. On the same day the London Olympic Organising Committee received an official protest against the fact that Dow Chemicals was to be a major sponsor of the 2012 games there. The protesters were a catholic mix of characters not usually sharing the same stage: politicians of all persuasions, former Gold medallists, Bollywood legends and the distinguished academic Noam Chomsky.

The timing of Jayakumar's report was interesting, coming as it did on the heels of the huge political debate currently raging around the Civil Nuclear Liability Bill. This American backed initiative states that in the case of an accident at Indian nuclear plants, U.S. companies involved would be responsible for only a small amount of any compensation due, Indian tax-payers bearing the bulk. Under the current international agreement, the Vienna Convention — supported by major players such as Germany, Japan, Finland and India — nuclear companies accept unlimited liability. In its opposition to Vienna, the US has the somewhat curious bedfellows of Morocco, Argentina and Rumania.

But Coke may yet laugh all the way to the bank. The universal tooth-dissolver was appointed as official beverage to both the Commonwealth Youth Games in Pune and the 19th Commonwealth Games held in Delhi in 2010. And in a lovely piece of irony, its Indian revenues may well be being boosted by an unlikely salesman. This is Baba Ramdev, a charismatic *hatha yoga* guru, whose weekly tv show draws an estimated 85 million viewers. A dedicated campaigner against corruption, the Baba recently formed what many sceptics would dub the ultimate oxymoron: a 'clean-up politics' political party. Be that as it may, Ramdev, who is also an avowed opponent of globalization, enthusiastically encourages his students and followers to buy Coke: "It is the best thing to clean your toilet with" he counsels.

41

The story of Lord Ganesh

THE SURREAL FORM of many Hindu deities has long perplexed Westerners, and shrouded the teachings of Hinduism with incomprehension. This confusion can be clearly seen in the descriptions of the earliest European travelers in the subcontinent. Many of these were Christian missionaries who were both horrified and frightened by the forms of the deities they encountered. To them the intermingling of animal and human observable in some deities was nothing less than demonic and it conjured up visions of the Biblical Apocalypse when the natural barriers between species are prophesied to become blurred. Time and again the word used in early travel accounts to describe Hindu images is 'monstrous', and the subtle and lofty symbolism of Indian iconography remained almost totally unsuspected by travelers, theologians and art historians alike until at least the 1920's. Even today, in the museum collections and auction houses of the world, Indian art continues to remain the poor relation to its less aesthetically challenging Japanese and Chinese cousins. A tasteful lacquered screen or scroll landscape may fit well into a conventional western interior but the emotional and formal power of an antique image of Vishnu or Shiva will blast everything else off the walls. If you are interested, a good history of European reactions to Indian art is Pitha Mitter's: *Much Maligned Monsters*.

And yet despite this track record, the Hindu deity that modern Westerners usually feel most drawn to is one of the strangest looking of all: Lord Ganesh. With his elephant's head and plumpy child's body, Ganesh is the god of good beginnings, protector of thresholds and the remover of obstacles. As such he should be invoked at the start of any project or undertaking. But how did such an important deity get such a bizarre form?

Lord Shiva and his wife Parvati were residing royally together on Mount Kailash in the high Himalayas. One day, Shiva had to leave unexpectedly. In his absence, Parvati went to take her daily bath and decided that she needed somebody to stand guard at the door so she wouldn't be disturbed. Scooping a handful of soapy foam from the water, she playfully fashioned a magical son from it, placing the boy outside the door with strict instructions not to let anybody in. Lord Shiva returned unexpectedly. On learning where his wife was, he went up to the bathroom to see her, only to be met by this young door guardian he had never seen before. The Lord demanded to be allowed in, but was refused entrance. He demanded again and was refused again. After the third refusal, Shiva lost his temper and with a bolt of fire from the third eye in the middle of his forehead blasted off the impudent little fellow's head. Hearing the commotion, Parvati came out of the bathroom and was distraught to see her son lying dead. She lambasted her husband who, full of contrition, vowed to restore the boy to life by giving him the head of the first creature he could find. As fate would have it, at that very moment one of the royal elephants came lumbering into the courtyard. With one blow of his mighty trident, Shiva removed its head and stuck it on to the little body. Thus was born Ganesh.

To compensate Parvati's magic son for such terrible treatment, Lord Shiva granted him the boon that henceforth, he would always have the right to be worshipped first of the gods, and so to this day, a Hindu worshipping other deities will first invoke Ganesh's blessings.

Ganesh is also the scribe of the scriptures. While they were being dictated to him by the celestial sage Vyasa, the tip of his stylus snapped off in mid-flow. So devoted was the little chap that he immediately broke off one of his tusks, dipped it in the ink and continued writing, in order that not a single word be lost. Thus he is also known as *Ekadanta* 'the one-toothed' and should always be portrayed with only one full tusk. In memory of this event, and as a tribute to him in his role as god of good beginnings, his name will be found inscribed at the start of any literary work by the devout.

As well as having the single tusk, an image of Ganesh should show him as four-armed and holding a conch shell or lotus, (the feminine symbol of creativity), a rosary (meditation) an axe (the power of discrimination) and a *modaka* or sweetened rice–ball. These, his preferred offerings, may well be responsible for his plumpiness. The multiple arms of Hindu deities allude to the many different aspects of the one Divine, which, with its unlimited power, is surely the archetypal multi-tasker.

Now, along with omnipotence goes omnipresence, so Ganesh's vehicle is always a rat or mouse. Strange logic? Well, as any Indian housewife knows, these little creatures can get in anywhere, in fact it is well-nigh impossible to keep them out. So what better symbols for the omnipresence of the divine spirit that animates all matter?

One of Ganesh's roles is as guardian of the threshold, so he should be placed above a lintel or near a door to protect the entrance; you will see him so positioned all over the subcontinent. Particularly popular among the mercantile communities in Western India, he is a shrewd little character. It is said that once he and his brother had a race to see who could go fastest around the world. His brother duly set off on the enormous voyage, while clever Ganesh stayed at home, quietly studying old texts on geography. Later he quoted these to prove that he had made the circuit, and so won the race. But if you go into a bank or a business and their Ganesh is turned to the wall, you might as well leave. They have gone bankrupt.

As the travel story suggests, Ganesh has a mischievous streak. In this mood he represents the universal myth-figure of 'the trickster', a mercurial and disruptive energy that can upset the very best laid plans. In many cultures the disruptive trickster is rudely phallic; Ganesh has no such risqué legends attached to him, but perhaps his trunk points in that direction. In fact, he belongs to a class of Hindu deities who are children or childlike — Krishna, Balaram, Subramanyam — and as such magically inspired; the stories of their naughty escapades symbolize the spontaneous and unpredictable nature the divine process. But there is another side to it. If one does not pay Ganesh his due attention, then his role as *Vinayaka* 'the remover of obstacles' may be reversed and he can actually place obstacles in your path. According to some accounts, the elephant headed one was originally a 'lord of misrule' who presided over a class of malevolent spirits called *vinayakas*. Ancient texts warn that if the *vinayakas* are displeased, "royal princes do not inherit, girls do not get good husbands, wives do not bear children and plans do not succeed".

So the next time you lose your car keys, spend half a day hunting for your glasses or cannot find that all important letter from the bank, say a prayer to Ganesh and see what happens. But will he be able to help if your gaze is set longingly on a throne, a spouse or having offspring — who knows these things?

42

The value of travel

THOSE WHO LOVE India will well understand the old saying 'travel broadens the mind', as opposed to armchair travel which tends only to broaden the behind. While many of the ancient epics tell the tale of a journey — the Odyssey, the Ramayana, Gilgamesh — modern travel writing is by and large a pretty disappointing genre, with but a few notable exceptions in each generation. Peter Fleming, Norman Douglas, Wilfred Thessiger, Robert Byron, Norman Lewis, Patrick Leigh Fermour, Colin Thubron are stellar examples in our time. Some writers, such as Andrew Harvey and Vikram Seth, produce a single travel masterpiece before moving on to other subjects, while others who don't forge a literary career out of their journeys often have worthwhile things to say about the process. Strangely, some of the most memorable of these come from America, a nation hardly noted nowadays for its adventurous travellers.

Let us start with some lines from the ever-pleasing pen of Mark Twain:

> "Travel is fatal to prejudice, bigotry and narrow-mindedness, and many of our people need it solely on these accounts. Broad, wholesome, charitable views of men and things cannot be acquired by vegetating in one little corner of the earth all one's lifetime".

The travelogue may be no great art form, but its inventor, the American photographer Burton Holmes, commented astutely:

> "One great advantage of travel is that you may enjoy all the satisfaction of possession without the responsibilities of ownership".

Ah, sweet music to the ears of itinerant Peter Pans everywhere!

A Frenchman, Anatole France, echoed Twain when he succinctly pinpointed the essence of travel as: "changing your opinions and prejudices". This transformative potential of voluntary dislocation was well described on many occasions by the sybaritic bohemian Henry Miller, who lived, wrote and painted in his adopted city Paris. As he said: "One's destination is never a place, but a new way of seeing things". A self-exiled American, Miller was in tune with an earlier, though considerably less Rabelaisian inhabitant of that city, Marcel Proust who despite (or perhaps because of) spending most of his time in bed, made the pertinent observation that we travel not in search of new sights, but of new eyes with which to see everything, old sights included.

The travelling life is not only socially disruptive, it was even the cause of the first murder, if, that is, we believe the biblical story that tells how the settled cultivator Cain killed his brother Abel because he was an uncivilised nomadic hunter. Us travellers have been on the run ever since. The perceptive itinerant Bruce Chatwin knew this only too well; in his collection of essays *The Anatomy of Restlessness*, he explores the human and social necessity of honouring the nomadic impulse, lauding it as a wild bloom all too easily stifled by inertia, habit and convention.

The ancient Indians certainly appreciated this spiritual value of travel. One of the vows made by the wandering mendicants known as *sadhus* ('good men') is to spend no more than three days in any one place. One such is said to live the life of a bee, moving from place to place in his search for spiritual nectar. Because of this he is known as *madhuvrata* ('one whose vow is to honey') a common Sanskrit name for that industrious little benefactor. In the *Aitreya Brahmana*, a text from 300 BC, Indra, King of the Gods, extols the virtues of the life of the road to a young seeker of truth:

> "There is no happiness for him who does not travel, Rohita!
> Thus we have heard. Living in the society of men,
> even the best man becomes a sinner
> Therefore, wander!
> The feet of the wanderer are like the flower, his soul is
> growing and reaping the fruit, and all his sins
> are destroyed by his fatigues in wandering,
> Therefore, wander!
> The fortune of him who is sitting, sits;
> It rises when he rises; it sleeps when he sleeps;
> It moves when he moves.
> Therefore, wander!"

And then there was the French-Algerian goalkeeper whose own life-journey encompassed the Nobel prize for literature. He saw travel as an initiation into the depths of the psyche: hauling anchor, disappearing from view and surrendering completely to the unknown. Such a vision will seem truly bizarre to the modern traveller who typifies our risk-averse society when he plots his carefully insured journey using Trip-advisor, clutches close her reassuringly familiar surroundings digitalised down into the latest electronic gadget and sends back a breathless stream of photos and comments to Facebook 'friends'. Albert Camus' radical perspective would not have won him a job in his local travel agents, but that's their loss. On real travel, as this piece from his *Notebooks* shows Camus is, and will surely remain, the master:

'When we are so far from our own country we are seized by a vague fear, and an instinctive desire to go back to the protection of old habits. This is the most obvious benefit of travel. At that moment we are feverish but also porous, so that the slightest touch makes us quiver to the depths of our being. We come across a cascade of light, and there is eternity. This is why we should not say that we travel for pleasure. There is no pleasure in travelling, and I look upon it more as an occasion for spiritual testing. If we understand by 'culture' the exercise of our most intimate sense — that of eternity — then we travel for 'culture'. Pleasure takes us away from ourselves in the same way as distraction, in Pascal's use of the word, takes us away from God. Travel, which is like a greater and a graver science, brings us back to ourselves'.

Perhaps it is fitting that such an intrepid traveller died in a car crash. Bon voyage, mon brave!

43

The versatile coconut

A RECENT ARTICLE in the Indian Express tells us of a super-smart Australian octopus that was discovered on the sea bed carrying around a coconut shell as a shield to protect itself. According to experts at Melbourne's Victoria Museum, this is the first recorded case of an invertebrate's using tools — a major indication of evolutionary intelligence originally thought to be the monopoly of humans, but now known to be found in other primates, mammals and birds.

Evolution has certainly favoured the survival of the coconut palm, as the nut can float on water for months and travel vast distances before washing up on some distant shore and happily germinating. Such mobility makes it impossible to trace its geographical origin, but *cocus nucifera* has certainly been cultivated here in India for over 4,000 years. South Indians in particular have always appreciated the nut's value: ancient texts laud it as the fruit of the *Kalpavriksha* 'the wish-fulfilling tree' and there is a hymn in Tamil listing no less than 108 beneficial uses.

A healthy palm can live as long as a human, and every part is used in some way or another in the daily life of coconut growing areas, of which Kerala is the foremost. The 'water' inside the tender green nut provides a refreshing and nutritious drink, high in vitamins and minerals, especially potassium. (This why the nuts were used as drips in wartime hospitals throughout south east Asia, providing hermetically sealed sources of instant rehydration and nourishment). The firm white flesh is also rich in nutrition and calories; grated and pulped it is a staple ingredient of local cuisine. Cut plant stems yield the sweet juice used in palm sugar, while the fermented sap produces toddy, the traditional local hooch. Once made, toddy should be quaffed within hours, as it soon goes off and the taste rapidly deteriorates to become vinegary.

Oil extracted from mature coconut plants has always been used for cooking; modern research shows it is high in good cholesterol and the constituent lauric acid gives the body instant energy by going straight to the liver, like a carbohydrate. Coconut oil is used everywhere: in chocolate, ice cream, pastries, ointments, toothpaste, soap, Ayurveda products, candles, dyes, paints, lubricants, plastics and even insecticides.

Pulped residue from the oil-extracting process is used as cattle fodder, stimulating healthy milk production in cows, and also as manure for trees and plants.

The palm leaves make roof-thatch and mats, and their midribs become good brooms, while the trunk of the tree is used in building and furniture making. Nut husks are a slow burning and virtually smokeless fuel. The shell is fashioned into cups, spoons and ladles; when burnt it produces a charcoal that is used in many filtering systems, from gas-masks to cigarettes! And their water-resistant qualities make two coconuts tied together an effective pair of water-wings for Malayali kids learning to swim. And then there is the coir. This outer, fibrous husk is soaked and beaten off the nut, cleaned and spun into yarn which is then used for rope, brushes, doormats, rugs, mattresses and pillows. Kerala accounts for 75% of India's coir production, the area around Alapuzha, formerly known as Allepey, being the centre of the industry.

The mythology surrounding the coconut is as ancient and dense as the groves in which it grows. A prime symbol of fertility, it is often kept in a shrine and presented to women desiring to conceive. One of its Sanskrit names is *narikela* 'man-fruit' and it has long been seen as a symbolic substitute for the human head. Traditionally carried into the temple on the worshipper's head (the highest and most spiritual part of the body) and then offered to the deity, the nut has the symbolic potency of a blood sacrifice but without the ritually polluting and low-caste associations of such a primal offering. If presented to an image, it must have its tuft intact, for this symbolizes the tuft of human hair. It is believed that the coconut, naturally sealed from impure influences, is the purest of offerings, and south Indian temples in particular are full of sudden cracking sounds as they are smashed on the stone floor, particularly in front of an image of Lord Ganesha to invoke his blessings of good luck. Such smashing should not take place in front of a pregnant woman however, as it is believed that a similar fate might transfer to the head of her unborn child. The coconut is also closely associated with Shiva, Lord of Transformation, as its three 'eyes' resemble the three-eyed deity.

There is a special day that perhaps dimly records the coconut's maritime travels. Each year the festival of *Narili purnima*, held on the full moon of the lunar month of *Shravana* (July–August), honours the coconut and the waters jointly. Sea and rivers are worshipped with *mantras* and coconuts thrown into them as offerings to the gods, particularly Varuna, Lord of the Deep. Traditionally, this festival was taken to mark the waning of the south-west monsoon storms and the resumption of trade and fishing along the west coast. And whereas the West launches a ship by smashing a bottle of champagne, abstemious Indians continue to prefer to use a coconut.

At it's most symbolic, the highly versatile fruit without a seed is taken to represent the entire range of existence. The rough outer husk is life's gross surface; the soft inner flesh the subtle, angelic realms; the pure milk the causal level and the inner space, the realm of pure unalloyed spirit. So, who knows, perhaps that defended Aussie octopus was also a bit of a metaphysician in his spare time?

44

'The Way of the Way'

IT HAS JUST been announced that an ancient yoga text called *Marga margasya* ('The Way of the Way') putatively dated mid-8thcentury AD, was recently discovered in a remote cave in the high Himalayan vastness. Experts believe this will shed invaluable light on the strange habits of Indian road users. The text appears here for the first time, translated from Sanskrit by our Cultural Director:

Verse 1: As we are in truth immortal spirit, so all road users should drive accordingly.

Verse 2: As we must respect the hierarchy of beings, so precedence must be given in this descending order: cows, elephants, water-buffalo, camels, heavy trucks, buses, official cars, light trucks, auto-rickshaws, private cars, motor bikes (carrying four or more), pedal rickshaws, goats, bicycles (carrying three or more), pigs, dogs, pedestrians.

Verse 3: As only the strong succeed, so for wheeled vehicles to slow is to show weakness, to brake is to fail and to stop is to be defeated.

Verse 4: As sound is divinely creative, so using the horn is compulsory, as:
a) Cars: Short blasts (urgent) indicate supremacy, e.g. in clearing dogs, rickshaws and pedestrians from the path. Long blasts (desperate) denote supplication, e.g. to oncoming truck: 'I am going too fast to stop, so unless you slow down we shall both die'. In extremis, they may be accompanied by flashing of headlights (frantic). Single blast (casual) means: 'I have just seen someone out of India's 1.2 billion inhabitants I recognise'; 'It is Lord Krishna's birthday next Tuesday' or 'I have not blown my horn for several minutes'.
b) Trucks and buses: All horn signals mean the same, i.e. 'I have a full weight of about 12.5 tons and have no intention of stopping for anything whatsoever, even if I could'. This signal may be accompanied by turning headlights on full in the face of approaching vehicle.

Verse 5: As the action of the enlightened is spontaneous, so all manoeuvres and evasive action shall be left to the last possible minute.

Verse 6: As guests are always to be honoured, so car occupants shall substitute safety belts with garlands of marigolds. These are to be kept unfastened at all times.

Verse 7: As we should always follow the Buddha's noble Middle Way, so traffic shall not drive on the left, nor on the right, but in the centre of the road.

Verse 8: As the round of samsara is an illusion, so roundabouts do not really exist in India. Apparent traffic islands in the middle of the road should be ignored as a sensory hallucination unhelpful to true understanding.

Verse 9: As all life is evolving, so overtaking is compulsory. Every moving vehicle is required to overtake every other moving vehicle, irrespective of whether it has just overtaken you. Overtaking should only occur in auspicious conditions, e.g. in the face of oncoming traffic, on blind bends, at junctions and in the middle of village and town centres on market day. No more than two inches should be allowed between you and the other vehicle; one inch in the case of bicycles and pedestrians.

Verse 10: As meditation and prayer are essential to the spiritual life, so all true seekers should close their eyes for regular periods of contemplation whilst at the wheel.

Verse 11: As life, when viewed aright, is one big celebration, so all vehicles should be painted up brightly on the outside, and be adorned with flowers, incense and images of the gods on the inside. For those with Mughal tastes, mirrored ceilings are also permitted.

Verse 12: As God moves in a mysterious way, so Kalki, the divine destroyer, may well come in the guise of a Kerala State Road Transport bus careering madly along National Highway 17.

Happy driving folks!

45

Too much monkey business?

IT TOOK ME a long time to come to like Hanumanji, one of the most popular of the Hindu deities. I don't know why exactly, there was something about that monkey-face and muscular body which didn't seem to have the charm of even Ganesh, the elephant-headed one, let alone the grace of the beautiful beings depicted in classical sculpture and painting. Anyway, whatever the reason, slowly the magic worked, and I have to say that the loyal servant of Ram and embodiment of devotion, enterprise and courage is a now a very firm favourite.

His popularity has been growing in North India too over the last few years. This is at least partly due to a holy man called Neem Karoli Baba, who you probably haven't heard of. Neither had many people, at least in the West, until he was discovered by a young American psychologist called Richard Alpert. Alpert had been one of the first to conduct clinical experiments using LSD, at a time when the psychiatric profession thought there might be great therapeutic potential in the drug. Under the influence of the most powerful psychotropic known, Alpert's experimentations soon lost all sense of propriety and along with his mentor, a charismatic Irish-American called Timothy Leary, the young phd was kicked off the faculty at Harvard. The genie was not only well and truly out of the bottle, but dancing, and the psychedelic 60's took off. As a result clinical trials were halted, LSD was banned and the two former boffins, having swapped their white lab-coats for brightly-patterned kaftans and beads, became US public enemies.

Leary spent the next few years being hounded by the American authorities in various parts of the world; Alpert retreated to India. While here he met Neem Karoli, became his devotee, was given the name Ram Dass and after serving his spiritual apprenticeship, was dispatched back to US to spread the message. The ex-Harvard psychologist has since become one of the most respected teachers on the New Age scene and his Hanuman Foundation does valuable work for the dying. The story of this, and much more besides, is told in a wonderful collection of anecdotes about his guru that Alpert edited: *Miracle of Love*. It is a fascinating glimpse, from a Western point of view that is respectful but not mindless, of what being around one of these 'god-men' (as the Indians call them) can be like.

Neem Karoli was such a great devotee of Ram that he was considered by many followers to be an incarnation of the paragon of devotion, Hanuman himself. This was no doubt partly aided by the fact that the man was double-jointed and could twist his body into extraordinarily simian contortions. This flexibility enabled his favourite pose of relaxation: reclining backwards on one elbow with one leg twisted over the other in the most unusual way. Neem Karoli had another unique identifying characteristic: he almost always wore nothing but an old plaid blanket wrapped around his body.

The guru established several ashrams dotted around north India, including one in the holy town of Vrindavan. He was staying there when he left the body in 1974. More than ten years later I was visiting the place with a group, one of whom was a woman who had never been to India before, knew nothing of the guru scene in general and, in particular, had certainly never heard of Neem Karoli. We happened to be standing together in the *darshan* hall looking at the photograph that hangs above the couch he always sat on. The picture shows him in his characteristic reclining pose and wearing the usual blanket. The woman asked if we could meet him. I told her that he had died some fifteen years previously. She looked at me incredulously. "But that's impossible, I've just seen him!" She went on to explain that as we were driving up to the ashram she had clearly seen him sitting on the pavement outside and had taken particular note of him because he was lying was in such an unusual position and was wearing just an old plaid blanket.

In the ashram there is a shrine containing an almost human-size marble statue of Hanuman. It was commissioned by the guru and it is said he was particularly fond of it. Although new, to my mind it radiates the most powerful energy, especially from the eyes that seem to look right through you. I have never seen a more lifelike piece of sculpture; it is positively eerie. The devotees believe this power derives from the fact that when Neem Karoli died, some portion of his spirit entered the image. On another occasion I was visiting the ashram with a different group, amongst which was a yoga teacher from England. A number of us were standing looking into the Hanuman shrine; I was up at the front by the railing, and some of the others were perhaps fifteen yards behind me. Suddenly I heard a commotion and turning round saw that the yoga teacher was flat on her back with people clustered around helping her.

She was very shocked and it took her a few minute to explain what had happened. According to her own account, she had made some comment to the effect of: "How stupid it is of these people to worship a monkey!" At that moment, so she said, she felt a blast of energy that came out of the shrine and struck her so forcibly on the chest that she was knocked off her feet backwards and onto the ground. Normally opinionated, she remained very quiet for the next couple of days.

In some temples dedicated to Hanuman, his troops are definitely in charge. This is particularly so in the foothills, where monkeys abound and Hanuman temples are correspondingly thick on the ground. There is a wonderfully wild place just above the town of Shimla, where the large intimidating males strut around the temple compound like aggressive security guards, accosting people who have come out of the shrine and frisking them for the *prasad* edibles that they are carrying. You have no choice but to hand it over.

That a temple to the monkey god should be dominated by the creatures is fair enough, but they also have a huge presence in the country's capital: there are estimated to be some 22,000 of them roaming Delhi's environs. They are particularly evident around New Delhi's Raisina Hill, where they throng the parliament buildings, a fact that has not gone unremarked by satirists. In 2007, New Delhi's Deputy Mayor died from head injuries sustained while trying to fight off a group which attacked him on the terrace of his home; more recently monkeys were blamed for breaking into the Ministry of Defence and carting off several armfuls of secret files which they sprinkled liberally around the government quarter. The simian situation reached a climax in the run up to the Commonwealth Games of 2010, when the city authorities were concerned that the proceedings could be disrupted and visitors attacked. Some visiting teams threatened to boycott the competition after complaining that their accommodation was overrun with animals and one South African competitor was shocked to discover a cobra in his room. The unwelcome visitor was blamed on the heavy monsoon rains that had caused flooding near the Games Village causing many snakes to seek drier land.

The solution was a delightfully Indian one. An elite squad of black-faced *langurs* was recruited and put on the government pay-roll as monkey police. The highly intelligent and fiercely territorial primates patrolled stadia and accommodation blocks to scare off not only other wild monkeys — *langurs* are larger and stronger than the resident strains of *rhesus macaque* — but the dogs and snakes as well. The simian cops did their job so well they are still deployed and seem to have the situation well in hand. You can see them riding pillion on the police bikes that cruise around the Raisina Hill complex.

Monkey business is also rife in Ahmedabad the former capital of Gujarat and a city with a large population of animal-loving Jains. Recently the army suspended the distribution *ladoos* and coconut *prasad* at a 400 year old Hanuman temple there, because troops of monkeys drawn by the food have been wreaking havoc at the nearby international airport and even grounding flights. It was while driving towards the city a few years ago that a small and freshly painted temple by the roadside drew my attention. I stopped, it was a charming place and I got into conversation with the officiating priest who told me his story.

He had been a senior manger for one of the large Indian banks, working in Delhi. One night he dreamt that Hanuman came to him with instructions to build at temple at a particular place in Gujarat. As he had never even visited that state, the location was unknown to him, and although he was a religious man and had taken the dream seriously, he could not see any way that he could do anything about it and so put it to the back of his mind. Not long after this, due to the unexpected early death of a colleague, the man was transferred to Ahmedabad to manage the local branch. Once settled down there, he had located the place mentioned in his dream and found it to be a small village on the main road into the city from the north. It was also a notorious accident blackspot. A few years later, an unforeseen and beneficial change in the bank's pension arrangements meant that it was possible for him to retire earlier than he had expected. He did so, and set about building a shrine at the spot he had been instructed. He and his wife moved there. When I met him, they were living very simply and happily in two or three rooms they had built at the back of the shrine; he officiated at the morning and evening *pujas* and the couple ran the temple together day-to-day. Many drivers now stop to give offerings and take blessings, and the accidents have completely stopped.

The pilgrimage town of Rishikesh is where the Ganges emerges into the plain and many holy men have their huts and caves on the eastern bank of the river. Not far from the Ram Jhula bridge I met a *sadhu* who was not only a devotee of Hanuman but even dressed as his chosen deity. Although the face make-up and monkey tail gave him a rather pantomimic air, the young man had a certain gravitas about him. He explained he was one of four disciples who had studied with a *guru* in

Punjab hills who had taught them the language of the monkeys and he was now travelling the country on perpetual pilgrimage. Unfortunately there were none of his fellow simians around so I was unable to test his abilities.

Sometime later I was in the bazaar and bought among other things a small but heavy brass image of Hanuman to give to a friend. The storekeeper wrapped it in newspaper and I put it in my shoulder bag along with some other stuff I had bought that including a couple of packages in shiny paper. On top lay a bunch of those wonderfully tasty little bananas that make it impossible to go back to the large cotton-wool frauds we generally have to put up with in Europe. At the far end of the east bank is a wooded area amidst which sits the long-deserted ashram of Maharishi Mahesh Yogi. It was here that the Beatles, the Beach Boys, Donovan and the rest came to study in the 60's. The area has a peaceful atmosphere and after wandering around a bit I decided to meditate for a few minutes, found a spot under a tree and sat down with my bag on the ground beside me. After some time I was disturbed by a commotion and opened my eyes to see a monkey gamboling away clutching something that he had taken from my bag. I assumed it would be the bananas, but on inspection found that he had ignored both them and the shiny packages, choosing instead the Hanuman image which was right at the bottom of the bag.

Such strange stories are not proof of anything, although believers might take them as such. But at the least, they surely illustrate that everyday reality is in truth a mystery, the deeper workings and interconnections of which go largely unnoticed. This is one reason why India, for me at least, has perennial fascination: she is the living museum of the human mind, a place where extraordinary things happen largely because people believe they can.

46

Transcendental medication

RECENT STUDIES HAVE shown that Transcendental Meditation (TM), all the rage during the Summer of Love — cue the Maharishi, Beatles, twangling sitar music and patchouli joss sticks — was by no means a passing fad. For one thing, it can halve the rate of heart attacks and strokes in patients with cardiovascular disease. The simple, natural technique, which seems to appeal to film directors — Clint Eastwood and David Lynch are two of its dedicated advocates — dramatically cut premature deaths in a nine-year study recently completed. 201 African–American men and women, average age 59, who suffered from narrowing of the heart arteries, were randomly assigned to practice T.M. or take health education classes with dietary and exercise advice. The classes had virtually no effect, but heart attacks, strokes and deaths fell by 47 per cent in the meditating group.

One of the latest of over 600 verified studies shows that meditation may switch off areas of the brain associated with daydreaming, anxiety, and certain psychiatric disorders such as autism and schizophrenia. "Meditation has been shown to help in a variety of health problems, such as helping people quit smoking, cope with cancer, and even prevent psoriasis," the study's lead author Judson A. Brewer of Yale University said, adding that meditation is well known to be linked with increased happiness.

His researchers used functional magnetic resonance imaging (fMRI) scans on experienced and novice meditators using three different meditation techniques. The results showed experienced meditators spontaneously exhibited interesting changes in brain functioning — especially in the default mode network (DMN) which involves parts of the brain such as the medial prefrontal and posterior cingulated cortices. Activity in these areas is associated with anxiety-based illnesses, attention deficit and hyperactivity disorder as well as plaque formation in Alzheimer's disease. Meditators showed clearly decreased activity. On the other hand, when the DMN network *was* active in experienced meditators, other brain areas linked to self-monitoring and cognitive control were found to be activated at the same time.

Significantly, these changes also continued outside of the meditation period, when the meditator was simply resting.

Confused? Well, in layman's terms, what the scientists are saying is that because their brain functioning is naturally suppressing self-centered and wandering thoughts, which in excess are strongly associated with autism and schizophrenia, meditators can focus on the present moment better. "Meditation's ability to help people stay in the moment has been part of philosophical and contemplative practices for thousands of years," Brewer said. "Conversely, the hallmark of many forms of mental illness is a preoccupation with one's own thoughts, a condition meditation seems to affect. This gives us some nice cues as to the neural mechanisms of how it might be working clinically."

What is more, it is now evident that meditators have more grey matter in the hippocampus, the part of the brain known to be important for learning and memory. A generalised reduction in stress level was also observable across the board, particularly with those practicing TM. To date more than 240 articles have been published in peer-reviewed scientific journals showing that the technique improves mental and physical health. Many of these studies were randomized clinical trials and meta-analyses. Recently, a charitable foundation set up by David Lynch received a $500,000 grant from the US government to teach the technique to 10,000 military veterans with post-traumatic stress.

At the furthest extreme of the self-healing spectrum, we now hear of a Tibetan lama who appears to have used meditation to cure himself of gangrene. Lama Phakyab Rinpoche arrived in America as a 37-year-old refugee with diabetes and a resulting circulatory deterioration so bad that his right foot and leg had already developed gangrene. He was examined by three different US doctors who shared one opinion: amputation. But the monk's mentor, the Dalai Lama, asked Rinpoche to forego an operation and instead utilize his skills at *tsa lung* meditation. Practitioners of this particular technique visualize a 'wind', a kind of life-energy that is one with the mind, moving down the central energy-channel in their spine clearing blockages and impurities before moving on to ever smaller energy-channels throughout the body. So, Rinpoche took no medicine but meditated all day, breaking only for meals.

In the early days of this regime, the putrid discharge from his leg ran black; a few months later it turned cloudy and bruising started to appear. The swelling increased and became more painful. The odor was sickening, he recalls, but he stoically continued and after nine months, the liquid leaking from his disabled leg began to run clear. The swelling went down. Soon he could put some weight on it. At ten months, he could walk again, at first with crutches. A short time later he was down to one crutch, and then, before even a year had passed, he was walking on his own. The tissue decomposition wasn't simply halted—his leg was back from the dead. The diabetes was gone as well.

Now a group of doctors at New York University has begun studying Rinpoche's brain. Team leader Dr. William Bushell, MIT affiliate and director of East-West Research for Tibet House in New York, says: "This is a cognitive-behavioral practice that present East-West science suggests may be more effective that any existing strictly Western medical intervention. It is not entirely clear from a Western perspective what the 'winds' are, but the scientific evidence suggests to me and others that the meditative process of directing imagery to both superficial and deep tissue sites in the body precipitates increased local blood flow, metabolic activity, and oxygenation." And so? "Such increases could in principle combat even powerful bacteria such as *staphylococcus aureus*, which not only can be the cause of gangrene, but is now often resistant to antibiotics" explains Bushell. His colleague in the study, one Dr. Josipovic adds: "What has become evident is that a great variety of meditation techniques, and the states of consciousness they engender, pose a considerable challenge for understanding them in terms of the established constructs of Western science."

So it looks as if it is time for Western medics to start re-thinking their habitual paradigms, because a new era of East-West understanding is dawning on the relationship of mind and matter. Oh, and come back Maharishi, all is forgiven!

47

Vis à vis visas

ONE OF THE health hazards of having anything to do with India is succumbing to 'Obdurate Babu Syndrome' (OBS). This is a quasi-medical condition brought on by repeated and protracted attempts to grapple with the government's mania for senseless regulation. The hapless victim of official OBStruction typically passes through consecutive stages of a downward spiral — from amusement to incredulity, to frustration, to annoyance, to downright anger. In severe cases, the condition can terminate in gibbering madness.

A frequent cause of OBS is the vexed question of visas. Those innocent travellers desiring to travel to and from the subcontinent often have their plans stymied by spats between the governments of the countries concerned. An example: some years ago I was involved in a scheme with an American company to make a tv film of some of India's ancient monuments. Part of the aim was to produce something that would boost India's woefully low tourist figures. Incredibly, the tiny island of Cyprus gets more tourists a year (i.e. over 2 million) than the entire subcontinent with all its extraordinary treasures. This is at least partly a result of woeful neglect by the Indian government of one of its greatest potential assets and the crashing mediocrity of successive Ministers of Tourism. One notable exception must be mentioned here: the statesman, scholar and environmentalist Dr. Karan Singh. A scion of the Kashmiri royal family, he illuminated the tourism post all too briefly in the 1970's and his *Autobiography*, as well as his many other writings, is well worth looking at.

Anyway, every attempt to get our filming visas was blocked. It eventually transpired that the brick wall was due to the US's having reversed its policy of issuing temporary visas to workers from places like India and the Philippines to allow them to enter the country and work while their immigration applications were pending. Now, all of these people were being forced to wait for final immigration approval — a process that could last 3 years — notwithstanding the adverse effects this would have on US businesses and health care costs. So, India was exacting revenge by denying US travellers visas to India. The film project duly died a death, not the first time I have fallen foul of visa spats. Even in relatively peaceful times, getting a visa from the UK required the marathon of dealing with the *ulta-pulta* visa department of the London High Commission. Here the unwary would queue for hours to submit payment with their forms — which still have to include a list of countries visited in the last ten years, two photos that cannot come from a regular photo-booth but are a special size (the office uses an American system) and the completion of two checklists — to be greeted on their eventual arrival at the counter with the news that only cash was accepted. This foretaste of actually being in India was recently replaced by having to negotiate the chronically unfriendly and tortuous Tourism Ministry website. No wonder the visa agents are doing a brisk business and may St. Christopher be thanked for their endeavours.

Terrorism has raised the visa nonsense to an altogether more heady level. In the wake of the Pune bombing, the Indian government went into knee-jerk mode and issued guidelines attempting to forestall the arrival of terrorists into the country — a hopeless task if ever there was one. These new regulations have been framed specifically in response to the antics of the American Islamist David Headley who, it has emerged, flitted effortlessly between Pakistan and the subcontinent many times over a period of years, setting up meetings and hatching terror plots. The government's response is quite extraordinary: non-resident Indians (NRI's) and tourists are to be banned from entering the country more than once in any two-month period.

Let's unpick this a bit. These days NRI's are a huge source of inward investment for India, many are retiring in their homeland while many others have to come here frequently in response to the manifold and complex demands incumbent on anyone who is part of an Indian family. The need to visit elderly or ailing parents twice in any two month period must be a frequent occurrence. And while the Tourism Ministry is energetically pushing 'Incredible India' around the globe, the Union Home Minister is now busy pulling in the opposite direction by limiting tourists and frustrating their ease of movement. For example: a common tourist itinerary involves flying into India, travelling around for a few days and then popping into neighbouring Shri Lanka, Nepal or Bhutan for a few more before a return to India and the return flight home. None of this will now be possible. Leaving aside the magical figure of two months that some *babu* must have plucked out of the air (why not one month, three, six even?) it gets even more illogical: the fact is that

Headley did all his travelling not on a tourist visa, but on a business one, and these are to remain as they were, with no extra policing.

A second wave of this brilliant initiative targeted foreign academics. Any scholar attending a conference on a topic that could be construed as controversial will no longer be granted a visa. This draconian measure applies principally to eight countries: China, Afghanistan, Sudan, Indonesia, Bangladesh, Iran, Iraq and Pakistan. Why scholars, why conferences? We all know that academia is a stressful place in these times of financial cuts, but do the *babus* in the Home Ministry really think that after failing to get tenure or having their latest publication rubbished in peer reviews, disgruntled scholars are going to rush to India in their long and envied vacations and start chucking bombs around? Anyway, if any academic really wishes to come here in order to create mayhem, all he or she has to do is come on a regular tourist visa, without mentioning any conference. And if, as is clear from the list of banned countries, it is Islamists that India is worried about, each and every one of the subcontinent's thousands of mosques and *madrasas* is a potential platform for incendiary rabble-rousing, no need to use the stately halls of academe.

In his reply to the barrage of press criticism, Ashim Khurana, Joint Secretary (Foreigners) Ministry of Home Affairs, attempted to clarify the muddle. Sublimely unaware of the irony, he pointed out that scholars from other countries are always free to visit India for conferences. All *(sic)* they have to do is: 1) get an invitation letter from the organiser, then 2) get event clearance from the Ministry of Home Affairs, then 3) get administrative approval of the nodal ministry, then 4) get political clearance from the Ministry of External Affairs and then 5) get clearance from the State Government/Union Territory concerned. So, nothing to it, then. Filling in all these forms and then waiting interminably for replies will surely keep those bomb-toting scholars occupied for months if not years. Mission accomplished.

Security imperatives cannot of course be ignored in a volatile international scenario that unfortunately looks like continuing far into the foreseeable future. No one should underestimate India's vulnerability to jihadism. But these recent and ill-thought out reactions will not stop one single terrorist. Meanwhile, those who genuinely care for the country — be they NRI, tourist or scholar — will pay a heavy price and the country herself will suffer various losses too, not least financial. What is more, the knock-on effect may well be a crisis in the health systems of many countries across the world, as already overworked medical staff resign in droves, unable to cope with the dramatic rise in cases of virulent OBS.

48

Waiting for the Mahatma

MAHATMA Gandhi's prayer-shawl has cast a long shadow over the subcontinent ever since it slipped from his shoulders as he was shot by a right-wing Hindu fanatic in early 1948, just six months after India celebrated her independence. Gandhiji's potent combination of wily pragmatism and ascetic sainthood — a brilliant deployment of 'strength through weakness' — had dovetailed perfectly with the national psyche. Indians tend to eschew outright conflict in favour of gaining the upper hand by subtler means, and while they are undoubtedly a pre-eminently religious people, they like their saints to be down to earth and display a certain shrewdness. This ensures that the holy one, while being exceptional, is still somehow one of the family, operating in a way that everyone can identify with.

The country is buzzing with a brace of dramas starring the latest in a long line of heirs-apparent to the Mahatma, and the stage is her perennial battle against the tyranny of corruption. First up was Baba Ramdev, a hugely popular yoga guru. I say 'was' because his largest mass demonstration to date ended in something of a farce recently when he was ignominiously forced to flee his protest camp amid scenes of police violence. Disguised as a woman, the guru was only apprehended when an alert cop noticed a bushy beard peeping out from under a floral face-scarf. Only a few days earlier he had arrived triumphantly in Delhi to begin his 'fast unto death' to demand the repatriation of the black money stashed abroad by India's corrupt rich. In 2006 this was already US$ 1,456 billion, 13 times the country's national debt and more than that hoarded by rest of the world put together.

Ramdev is currently the most famous guru in north India; from his base beside the sacred Ganges at Haridwar in the foothills of the Himalayas he controls a yoga and meditation network said to be worth £150m. The penultimate act of the protest drama, set in a third-floor suite of a smart Delhi hotel, featured a pair of cabinet ministers pleading with the saffron-robed holy man not to continue the hunger strike he had launched. But the guru was not for turning; after five additional hours of supposedly secret negotiations at the Claridges Hotel, Ramdev was photographed sweeping away in an entourage of vehicles. His destination? The Ram

Lila field on the edge of the old city, where thousands of his supporters awaited him in a vast yoga camp complete with 50 doctors, an intensive care unit and a state-of-the-art media centre. The government then admitted defeat by confirming it had been unable to reach agreement with him on his demands.

In the language of north India, the yoga camp was initially quite a *tamasha*, a good-natured celebration as political gatherings often are here. However, when 100,000 extra supporters flocked to the scene, the government panicked and sent in police with sticks and tear gas. The highly unpopular Home Minister, P. Chidambaram, himself under the spotlight for corruption in a massive telecom scam, is rumoured to have ordered the charge. Beating up and gassing peaceful anti-corruption protestors while the cameras roll is not the most sensible public-relations policy and it left Congress party leader Manmohan Singh's unpopular administration looking ever more beleaguered.

Ramdev shot to fame ten years ago when his yoga instruction and ayurvedic medical treatments were broadcast on Indian tv; today his early morning broadcasts enjoy a daily audience of at least 20 million in India alone. Viewers were attracted as much by his celibate healthiness and robust sense of humour as by his stress-busting breathing exercises. Since then, he has increasingly advanced views that are nationalistic and political. Some of them do not appear clearly thought through. One such is the promotion of education in Hindi rather than English, a change which would not do much for India's linguistic pre-eminence over China in global business and would also infuriate the huge number of south Indians who have always disliked Hindi which they see as an alien symbol of north Indian dominance. Another, the scrapping of 500 and 1,000 rupee notes, may seem more eccentric than revolutionary to the eyes of the outside world. The guru abhors multinational corporations and believes the WHO is an American 'pharma–conspiracy'. His aim is to free India from the corrupting influence of the West in all its guises; he once memorably counselled his followers to "buy Coke because it is the best thing to clean your toilets with".

Anyway, Ramdev certainly has many followers and they do not all come, as he does, from the disadvantaged poor. The growing middle classes, mistrustful of the entrenched élite, are increasingly frustrated with the country's endemic corruption. But even the opposition BJP party is wary of the turmoil that too much of the yogi could unleash on the country's fragile parliamentary democracy. Predictably, his opponents claim that he is a media-puffed fraud peddling quack cures for everything from Aids to cancer, and they mutter their suspicions about the finances of his charitable trust, along with the recent acquisition of Little Cumbrae. This is a Scottish island worth a not so little £2m, a gift from well-heeled devotees that is planned to be a spiritual centre in a part of the world which traditionally prefers its spirit tawny, neat and definitely without ice.

The yogi has now retreated to his ashram in the holy city of Haridwar, and it currently looks as if his crusade will need a miracle worthy of Lazarus if it is to revive. But we may not have heard the end of this rather appealing and surely sincere character. He has certainly tuned into a huge and widespread popular desire for reform — witness one of his quoted supporters, a Mr. Kalu Ram, who had cycled all the way from the state of Gujarat to join the Ram Lila ground protest. The 600 miles took him eight days. "I am very worried about the level of corruption. I have to deal with it every day," said the 67-year-old Mr Ram, who works as a cook. "Sometimes I feel I could be like Nathuram Godse to get rid of corruption in India." (A significant, if muddled, reference this: Godse was the Hindu nationalist who assassinated Gandhi.) As the Financial Times recently warned its readers, we should never underestimate 'the timeless power of the Hindu ascetic to create turmoil in the world's largest democracy'.

Prescient words. No sooner had Ramdev exited stage left than another candidate for the Mahatma's legacy strode into the limelight to take his place: cue Mr. Anna Hazare. Long known in India but new to the West, Mr. Hazare is an endearing 74 year old anti-corruption campaigner who wears the Gandhian white *khadi* cotton and has also had recourse to a hunger fast, and a more successful one than the yogi's, it turns out. An avowed follower of the Mahatma, Hazare's enormous popularity had galvanised hundreds of thousands of people at various sites across the sub-continent, including sit-down protests outside the houses of prominent Congress politicians in the capital. Much of Mumbai was paralysed by strikes and demonstrations and leading Bollywood actors swung behind the movement, donning the traditional white cotton Congress caps that are its symbol. Many supporters also went on sympathetic hunger strike to support Anna, whose name is a nice irony, as *anna* means 'food' in Sanskrit and some Indian languages.

Irony or not, this time the old weapon of not eating proved invincible. After 13 days the Singh government which had originally arrested Hazare, then dismissed him as an anarchist, caved in as parliament backed anti-graft legislation that met many of his demands. It agreed to scrutinise the lower tiers of bureaucracy, set up a national and independent ombudsman to monitor bribery and corruption and establish a citizens' charter. But they should be warned. "I haven't given up the fast, only suspended it" Hazare told the press as he sipped coconut water and honey to ease his system back to normal. "It will really end when parliament passes the bill and there is genuine reform".

The fasting crusader is not without his critics. Most strident is the Booker winning novelist turned social activist Arundhati Roy, who, since his arrival on the scene, has been in danger of being knocked off the front pages. Arundhati means 'the unobstructed' and Ms. Roy has certainly been uninhibited in her criticisms, deploring Hazare's 'nationalism' and the fact that his supporters wave the Indian flag. "While his means may be Gandhian, his demands are certainly not" she wrote in The Hindu, the country's main left-leaning newspaper. She warned the ombudsman would merely replicate the "bloated, unaccountable and corrupt" administration, and end up creating "two oligarchies instead of one". Inevitably, the unclean left hand of the Hindu right is suspected of pulling the puppet's strings behind the scenes. "Certainly Anna Hazare was picked up and propped up as a sort of saint of the masses, but he wasn't driving the movement, he wasn't the brains behind the movement," hinted Roy darkly. Her criticisms have been echoed by other commentators.

Meanwhile, on the other side of the world, Gujarati-born Lord Bhikhu Parekh, New Labour party peer and academic big-wig, warned the London audience at his 2011 Jawaharlal Nehru Memorial Lecture that unelected leaders like Hazare "threaten parliamentary democracy because they have no electoral mandate but could have plenty of self-serving agendas". Parekh's words may raise a hollow laugh amongst those Indians who actually live in India. The world's largest democracy has elected representatives a-plenty, and about the only thing they have consistently delivered is a new benchmark in what it means to be 'self-serving'. Under its elected politicians the country has suffered widespread corruption, lack of accountability, disregard for democratic institutions, a media in hock to corporate consensus and despite a generally impressive economic growth, an ever-growing disparity between rich and poor. For the noble lord to dismiss Hazare's huge popular support because it doesn't conform to some academic model of democracy must strike the average Indian as an opinion floating dizzily down from an ermine-lined cloud-cuckoo land.

Inevitably, there is a Muslim dimension to the Hazare saga and it is also discordant. As his profile picked up steam, the venerable campaigner was forced to retract an earlier statement of support for Narendra Modi, Chief Minister of Gujarat, a right-wing Hindu who is accused of instigating anti-Muslim pogroms there in 2002. But as his campaign rolls on, this down to earth neo-Gandhian must learn to be a bit more politically savvy if he wants to succeed. When the Union agriculture minister was attacked by a youth at a Delhi rally recently, Hazare went on record as saying that it was "just one slap" and anyway the minister deserved to be harassed as he had an "old habit of protecting corrupt people". Then came his policy for dealing with persistent drunkards, an approach that has apparently proved effective his native village in Maharashtra. "After warning him thrice if he again drinks, then we will take him to temple and he has to swear to God that he won't drink in future" explains tea-totaller Hazare. "If he still continues to drink, he is tied to a pole outside the temple and given a beating". The forthright honesty of such opinions renders them politically incorrect, yet they seem unlikely to derail Hazare's bandwagon, at least for the moment. Simply put, Indians are heartily sick and tired of corruption and they want a visible sign that something can, or at least might, be done about it.

And one may have already arrived. News has just come in that one of the country's most powerful mining barons, whose political clout and huge wealth have made him a notorious national figure, was arrested in a raid on his offices which yielded about £750,000 in cash and over 20 kilos of gold bars. The tycoon, G. Janardhana Reddy, is based in the district of Bellary in Karnataka, a big mining state. Reddy and his brothers, after working their way up from delivering leaflets by scooter for the B.J.P. to becoming power-brokers and fund providers for the party, held the lucrative government leases in their well-greased palms. N. Santosh Hedge, the independent ombudsman who has spent more than two years investigating the illegal mining said to have cost the state over £2.25 billion in lost tax revenues, announced: 'It was a mafia-like system. That district has become the republic of Bellary; it is not part of India'.

The problem is endemic. To talk of 'corruption' assumes that the system is basically honest with occasional and regrettable aberrations. But if corruption is the universal norm, the essential dynamic rule that everyone understands and abides by and not just the exception, where do you start? And if corruption really was ousted, might not the governance of the Indian body politic, like some ancient and rickety engine deprived of its sticky black oil, just seize up and grind to a halt? Indeed, if the whole system is rickety enough, then corruption actually becomes the only means of opportunity to millions otherwise deprived of it.

Asked recently about the possibilities of reform, the Prime Minister said he was "open to a reasoned debate" but added that in the fight to eradicate institutionalised corruption there was "no single solution". A pregnant phrase, that. In fact, the only single solution would be if the Mahatma were to re-incarnate, bind the country together with his hallowed prayer shawl and banish the venal and self-serving bureaucrats with a wave of his sanctified hand. Whether the drip-effect of assorted Ramdevs and Hazares will be enough to do the same remains to be seen, but at least it's a start.

49

Water, water everywhere

It was W.C. Fields — film actor, wit and serious tippler — who declared: "I wouldn't dream of drinking water because of the disgusting things fish do in it". But despite the great man's reservations, we humans are watery creatures, and we actually thrive on the stuff. Water composes 75 per cent of the brain, helps carry nutrients and oxygen to cells, regulates body temperature, moistens oxygen for breathing, helps convert food into energy, protects and cushions the vital organs, helps the body absorb nutrients, makes up 75 per cent of our muscles, cushions our joints, accounts for 22 per cent of our bones, removes waste from the body and makes up 63 per cent of the blood. Phew!

Generally it takes only a 1% depletion of our body water to make us feel thirsty but in Kerala's climate added regular intake of fluid is very necessary. Ayurveda extols its medicinal properties. As a general tip, drink 2 glasses of water after waking up, it helps activate the internal organs. A glass of water before taking a bath helps lower blood pressure, whereas a glass before sleep helps avoid the chances of a nocturnal stroke or heart attack.

All our water here at The Hermitage is purified by the latest method of reverse-osmosis and we refuse all bottled water as part of our eco-policy. Over 50 companies sell bottled water in Kerala; none of it is real mineral water, none of it is tested for safety and not one single bottle is recyclable. By not using bottled water we also avoid adding well over a hundred plastic bottles each day to Kerala's already mountainous rubbish problem.

Some of the water in your room is kept in a copper container and becomes subtly charged with that mineral's properties. High in silica and selenium, it will strengthen the heart and immune system and detoxify the liver. Ayurveda also suggests we sip warm water throughout the day, so enjoy the herbal waters we serve at the start of each meal, (cumin at breakfast, *sappan* bark at lunch, cinnamon at dinner). They purify the blood and aid digestion. But remember to avoid iced water at meals — by extinguishing the digestive 'fire' it inhibits digestion, leading to storage of toxins in the system, subsequent obesity and eventual ill-health.

Moreover, it seems water has hidden depths. A batch of new discoveries suggests that manipulating an individual water molecule's interactions with its neighbours could help solve some of the world's thorny problems in both agriculture and health. And for a more mystical angle, check out the work of Masaru Emoto, a creative and visionary Japanese researcher whose book, *The Message from Water* offers factual evidence that human vibrational energy — thoughts, words, feelings — and also music, all affect the molecular structure of water. The photos he has taken showing these effects are awesome. Given that water comprises over seventy percent of a mature human body and covers the same amount of our planet, the implications for the power of collective consciousness are intriguing. It seems that the quality of our life is directly connected to the quality of our water.

Back to W.C.F., who claimed that he had only once in his life turned down the offer of a drink and that was when he had misunderstood the question. Just in case it was not asked though, he always took a generous hip-flask on set to ease him through the day's work, referring to it as 'my orange juice.' One day while he was temporarily off set, some of the film crew emptied out the scotch and filled the flask up with orange juice. On taking his next swig, the notoriously irascible Fields exploded. "Somebody's put orange juice in my orange juice!" he thundered.

50

We love you Jairam!

THESE DAYS POLITICIANS are hardly the most popular of celebrities anywhere in the world. Here in India they come a very long way indeed behind gyrating Bollywood stars and designer-stubbled cricketers, but there is currently at least one exception to this rule. Enter the highly personable and rather flamboyant Jairam Ramesh, currently Union Minister of State for Environment and Forests with a spare-time role writing speeches for the two latest representatives of the Nehru dynasty, Sonia Gandhi and her son Rahul, general secretary of the Congress party.

What first endeared people to Jairam was his resolute stance against the threat of GM food. Last year he boldly declared a national moratorium on *Bt Brinjal*—a transgenic aubergine hybrid being touted by a company called Mahyco, which it turns out, is a subsidiary of our old friend Monsanto. It was a bold position to take, as all over the developing world the big guns are lining up behind the cause of genetically modified and bio-fortified crops. In India the National academy of Sciences sees new breeds such as vitamin A enriched 'Golden Rice' or iron-enriched wheat as being the answer to the problems of feeding growing and hungry populations in the coming years of climate change and possible water shortage. By 2050 the global population will surpass 9 billion, and it will require almost a doubling of agricultural output to fill all those bellies, many of them in India of course.

So much for the figures. But Jairam is in touch with the feelings of the people, and was widely lauded for standing up for consumers against the suspect motives of many of India's GM advocates. Chief villain here was Prithiviraj Chavan, Science and Technology Minister, who pushed for *Bt Brinjal* in a letter that, it transpired, he had copied word for word from a study funded by interested biotech seed companies, including Monsanto. Now he has been pushing for a new bill, which will approve GM foods to enter India without any checks. This, say his critics, is trampling the rights of elected representatives and forcing GM foods on all of us.

To date, the Indian government has vacillated on GM, only deigning to consider the merits of a public debate when controversy threatened to grow into crisis. But too few tests and a general lack of clarity on the subject, plus chronic suspicion of international corporate attempts to control food production, storage and supply, had many farmers and activists worried. Vigorous local, internet and NGO campaigns led half a dozen states to ban the transgenic *brinjal* — and possibly all future GM crops — from their fields. As the subcontinent lacks an adequate labelling regime, once a GM vegetable enters local markets, there would be no way of distinguishing it from the natural variety, effectively leaving the consumer no choice. One spin-off from this situation would be that indigenous healthcare traditions were compromised; aubergine, the current cause célèbre, is used extensively in Ayurvedic medicines.

India knows corporate seed-greed well. She fought a long and finally successful battle against multinational attempts to patent the *neem*, a tree whose leaves have been a staple in folk medicine and traditional healthcare for millennia. In 2006 over 2,000 sheep died in the southern state of Andhra Pradesh after grazing in a field of GM cotton for a week. Then it was shown that the engineered cotton yields 15% less per acre than a natural crop and needs up to ten times more fertilizer. Finally it emerged that contrary to its maker's claims, GM cotton was not pest-resistant at all, falling prey to cotton's old enemy, the pink boll weevil. Even Monsanto admitted "more research is needed."

Announcing the moratorium on GM, Jairam counseled India patiently to observe the long-term effects of genetic engineering in those countries so assiduously pushing it around the world. The ban will last "till such time independent studies establish, to the satisfaction of both the public and professionals, the safety of the product from the point of view of its long-term impact on human health and environment, including the rich genetic wealth existing in *brinjal* in our country."

Another battle involved Vedanta, a UK based mining company, and its plan to mine bauxalite, a key component of aluminum, in the Niyamgiri hills of Orissa. The hills are home to the 10,000-strong Dongria Kondh tribe, an aboriginal people who worship them as divine. According to eco-campaigners, the mine would entail destruction of the environment and water sources; human rights critics talked of the annihilation of the tribals' livelihood and culture. Vedanta refused to answer questions from investors, media and pressure groups so many shareholders, including the Church of England and the state pension funds of Norway and the Netherlands, sold out in protest. Last year Jairam lambasted Vedanta's project, stating bluntly: "There has been a very serious violation of laws. Therefore the project cannot go ahead". In a country where the rights of small groups have routinely been squashed by multinational muscle and environmental consequences have never figured in rapacious business calculations, such a high-level condemnation is highly significant.

These decisions are important pieces of a very complex jigsaw. On the threshold of unprecedented economic growth, India could easily continue its present habit of blindly following deeply flawed Western models. Think 'crony capitalism', where the government gets into bed with powerful business elites to create favourable monopolies, and its cousin 'phoney capitalism', such as is found in Russia and the oil-rich Gulf, where the classic principle of a steady return on invested capital has been ditched in favour of sudden and momentous windfall profits for the opportunistic few. Given the Himalayan depth of the average politician's pockets, either option would be a disaster here.

Just before Christmas 2010, Jairam David struck another blow against Corporate Goliath by announcing that fiscal incentives must be created to encourage sustainable development. The current bias towards only considering financial returns must in future be tempered with concern for energy and water conservation, and business must pay attention to the protection and preservation of natural resources. What is more, Ramesh has recently broken new ground by committing India to legally binding carbon emissions. As the country hurtles headlong towards ever greater and much-needed growth, such tempering wisdom is as timely as it is rare. Keep up the good work Jairam, we love you!

51

Young India shining

A LITTLE OVER a year ago video footage emerged from a remote village in northern India. It showed a young girl receiving surgery to separate her fingers, which had been badly burned and fused together when her family's paraffin cooker blew up. A not uncommon accident, so why did news of this operation make headlines around the world? Because it was performed by a 7-year-old boy. His name is Akrit Jaswal.

The boy-surgeon apparently developed a passion for science and anatomy at an early age, assembling a childhood library of medical textbooks. Doctors at local hospitals took notice and started allowing him to observe operations when he was only 6 years old. Inspired by what he saw, Akrit continued to read everything he could on the topic, and word of his prowess began to spread. So when the impoverished rural family heard about his unusual medical knowledge, they asked if he would operate on their daughter's mangled hand for free. He agreed and her surgery was a complete success. After the operation, Akrit was hailed as something of a medical genius in India; neighbours and even strangers began flocking to him for advice and treatment.

Now all of 13 years old, Akrit, who has an IQ of 146, has been studying at the nearby Punjab University since he was 11, which makes him the youngest student ever to attend an Indian university. The same year he started there, he was also invited to Imperial College in London to exchange ideas with scientists working on the cutting edge (no pun intended) of medical research. Akrit says he has dozens of medical ideas, but he's currently focused on developing a cure for cancer. "I've developed a concept called oral gene therapy on the basis of my research and my theories," he says. "I'm quite dedicated towards working on this mechanism. Going to hospitals since the age of 6 I have seen, first-hand, many people suffering from pain," he adds. "I get very sad, and so that's the main motive of my passion about medicine, my passion about cancer." What a heart-warming story. Congratulations, Akrit, and don't let anyone or anything deter you from following your passion.

Another young Indian in the news hails from the other end of the subcontinent, down here in Kerala in fact. C.V. Midhun, the son of a brahmin temple priest and a teacher and now a second year physics student, has had the temerity to challenge Stephen Hawking's black hole theory. The venerable Cambridge boffin has long predicted that when the nano-particles called protons collide then a black hole, sucking in all surrounding matter, is produced.

Young Midhun is not so sure. His argument was, by the standards of high energy physics anyway, a simple one: first you measure the energy generated by the sun, and then you compare it with that coming out of a particle collision. His conclusion? "The energy of the sun's cosmic rays has been found to be much more than that of the cosmic rays from particle collision. As there is no black hole in the sun, it is unlikely there will be a black hole when subatomic particles collide inside a particle accelerator".

Well, this all sounds fair enough (to this ignorant layman at least) and the scientific establishment, which has always known that the inventive ideas belong to the young, is delighted. Midhun has been invited to become part of the world-leading experimental team at CERN in Switzerland. His parents are of course very proud and no doubt his mother will be busily selecting assorted thick woolies to prepare Midhun for the alarming lack of Keralite sun in northern Europe. Two shining young Indians; in both these cases, and no doubt countless others, watch this space...

Watch out for *More Views from an Indian Bus* to be published soon...